Another Garden

Another Garden

Tanka Writings

Jeffrey Woodward

TOURNESOL

DETROIT • 2013

Published by Tournesol Books
PO Box 441152
Detroit, MI 48244-1152
www.tournesolbooks.com

ISBN: 978-0615892511

Cover and interior book design by the author.

Cover image: Paul Cézanne, *Étude de Pomme*, watercolor and pencil, circa 1890.

Printed in the United States of America

10 9 8 7 6 5 4 3 2 1

See pages 177-178 for an acknowledgment of the prior publications of those tanka writings included in this book.

I was raised in a remote part of the country . . .

The Sarashina Diary

CONTENTS

A Deck of Cards

Partial Census

Blue Flag

The Simple News

Lagniappe: Two Essays, One Interview

A Deck of Cards

Graceful Willow

Sixteen perhaps, auburn hair pulled back tightly in a bun, a trace of cranberry lipstick that her mother very likely did not approve. Forsythia aflame and, before the bench by the river where she leans to write, tulips opening. Her elegant and practiced cursive is like that of the current—flowing on and on. She is too young, certainly, to guard so many secrets. And her diary—would it possess the patience to receive them?

the willow is green
young and eager to become
for wind and water
the pliable plaything of
each breath and eddy of spring

The Silence That Inhabits Houses

High summer on the Florida coast, shut indoors well-before noon to evade the burning sun, seated alone at the table with Pierre Schneider's exuberant monograph on Matisse, I renew my reading late in the master's career—an elegiac digression on the aged painter's surgery, convalescence and recovery of sufficient strength, for a brief period, to paint a few last summary canvases. Introduction of black is the key to the late intensity of color, the foil for his generous palette, the counterpoint for his final surrender to the light's largesse.

I turn the page, then, to discover *Le silence habité des maisons*. How the yellow of that day in 1947 on the French Riviera dominates the window at the right of the painting. The coastal foliage and far sky, beyond the billowing cumulus, lavishly spend green and blue on the pair of readers of the large book at rest on a table near a vase—readers without faces, a book without type, flowers without definition, bare outlines in a yellow borrowed from the window, obliterated faces and bodies in a blue borrowed from on high within a dominant black interior.

The very anonymity of the readers is comforting; the book that offers nothing legible, inexplicably so. I, too, sit in a room of shifting shadow, well away from an incandescent window that opens onto a day uncannily like that one in 1947, in an interior that closely resembles that of the French painter in his villa.

yellow afternoon
flares at the window—and fronds
of royal palm, too . . .
barely does that sun blush on
the book or reader shut within

The Girl from Shanghai

gazing intently
at the many pointed rays
of these starry emblems
no less than the sown heavens
the chicory in bloom

That is where I first observed Mei Lin, there on a midsummer day in a city park, a young Chinese girl with my son of like age, fellow resident of his at the group home, similarly troubled but with the added barrier of language. No one spoke her native Mandarin at the residence and Mei Lin had only a smattering of English at her command.

That is where they stood, my son and the young girl from Shanghai, surrounded on all sides by that pale blue sprinkling of flowers that clings to the shoulder of a road, to the cracked macadam of an out-of-the-way or dead-end alley, to the vacant or abandoned lot, to the waste places and disturbed sites of transient human habitation.

I first discovered Mei Lin some days earlier in a spiral notebook left open on my son's bed. Page after page of meticulous but masculinely drawn Chinese characters were there underlined by an English paraphrase in a feminine hand—the girl from Shanghai teaching my son Mandarin, my son teaching the girl English.

No one at the home could tell me how or when Mei Lin had arrived. Everyone agreed that she did so in her current state. Her world was elsewhere—not in North America, certainly, and perhaps not in Shanghai. Her world was my son's, and my son's was hers: for the time being—in the heat of a summer day, under a cloudless sky, there with the wildflowers.

a wayfarer
or stowaway
from Eurasia
the chicory is blue on
either side of the road

Souvenir

light falls from her hair
onto a gold necklace
and lapis lazuli
a carafe's close shadow
of cerulean hue

reminding me in autumn in this popular pub of you in high
summer here at my side your eastern city far behind

I leave that shimmering aura where it lingers with an
admirer about a corner table but nevertheless your shadow
follows me somehow into October into a sudden evening
into a windy street

if I turn back now
and look to the east
the heavens blacken
where tonight you lie at ease
beside another

The Late Afternoon of Basil O

twirling
a number 2
soft-lead pencil
national school
bus yellow

the paper punch
and tinny stapler
near at hand
stodgily gray but as suave
as the business suit, the day

found at
the bottom
of a box
the end of a long
paperclip chain

Frosted glass on the wooden door entrance, the name Basil O (the concluding block letters worn away) forms a partial arch with a title, "Certified Accountant," for a clear foundation. Read that backward inscription then from the cloistered interior of the office or, if so disposed, right the whole by turning away to face the mirror on the opposite wall.

To the left, a standard nondescript desk and tools of the numbers trade, an oblong window *behind* (a view of an adjacent third story brownstone walkup and our window's double—who can surmise what they do over there?) and a pair of simple chairs for the clientele *before*. To the right, twin filing cabinets, antiquated water cooler and one coat-rack minus coat or hat . . .

one hundred
round head
brass brads
to the box—
size, number 5

buried under
a dusty stack
of confidential files
the calculator
that adds up to nothing

. . . or one coat-rack minus coat and hat. The severe angle of the light of day on the wall to your right, the clock that *says* and the clock that *said* long ago a quarter to five now partially cloaked in shadow, the vacancy of the scene is palpable in the faint warmth of the sun on the back of the hand that opens, that closes a door.

the volume on
the office phone
readjusted
listen closely
and it may ring

Photograph at 19

my hair to my shoulder a thin goatee a thin moustache
under small 1930s–style round tortoise-shell frames and my
grandfather's tweed flat cap and my U.S. regulation bomber
jacket with worn zippers and cracked leather ransomed
from the Salvation Army

      the wind is caught up
      where the light in the photo
      falls on my hair
      the jacket left open
      inviting spring

      what little remains
      of an old five-and-dime
      splintered boards and bricks
      in a heap behind me and
      the ragged half of a wall

the cap at 19 like a shadow like a shade of Kerouac on
Route 66 which I also know but no one steps twice onto
the same road

the tortoise-shell too self-consciously like Comrade
Trotsky a minor antithesis perhaps lines my jacket
uncovered where a paperback peeks from my pocket what
other than the *Illuminations* of Rimbaud but let us confess
our contradiction let us turn to dialectic whether or not
Rimbaud ever truly mounted a barricade in the Paris
Commune wasn't that Rimbaud French schoolboy in the
daguerreotype on the New Directions cover some years
before he crossed over to the other side to skim a franc here
a franc there from a caravan hauling guns Rimbaud reputed
crony of traders marching slaves to market in Harar in East
Africa Rimbaud with a billet in Aden not Eden

in the days before the truth found itself in exile in the days
before *Pravda* and Stalin collected farmers for Siberia or
before peasants harvested famine before a pick-axe found
Coyoacán or an Enola Gay fly-boy a bomber jacket

           just back by way
           of Hoboken & Hackensack
           back from a brief stay
           in that drafty warren
           in the East Village

I look very bookish
in my bookish glasses
squinting myopically
into somebody's camera
while waiting for spring

underlined in my copy of Rimbaud *Je est un autre* a French schoolboy's letter and manifesto for a systematic derangement of the five senses

and what of Trotsky with *Las Dos Fridas* in Coyoacán where Frida Kahlo is left alone to hold her own hand

and what of so-and-so and somebody's plan to meet on or about May Day at the Cliff House or perhaps on Russian Hill to view the Golden Gate

underlined in my Rimbaud *à son état primitif de fils du Soleil* license enough to seek to restore that child of the Sun that primitive state

Resident Angel—Tanka

spring begins
unexpectedly
with the letter
of a stranger
from afar

she lies on her back
in the cool grass awhile
a winding stream
nearby parallel
a cloud in the sky

the resident angel
perpetually
hands folded in prayer
never shall unfurl her wings
of stone or test the air

though the mayfly
may not live to
love tomorrow
in loving tonight he
outlives your vow

on the river road
in possession of
a modest dwelling
this retiring pair
of weeping willows

that an ancient one
or two were slyly known
to lie in the grass
shall not make me love it more
nor call a stone my pillow

piling by piling
the wooden dock
sags a little
and deep in its midday shade
a largemouth's shadow

sorting through
the mélange of what the sea
tosses back ashore
nothing but plain air within
the blue of a bottle

my taste once inclined
through a long dry season
to stone and water . . .
but now it is there, for love,
in the tangles of your hair

the hull wants caulk
and yet invitingly
the punt waits at the dock
and points the way
to deeper water

lying on her side
pretty chin propped up
in her hand she
looks girlishly innocent
and yet she lies

I look to the pine
that leans severely
its root exposed by
a vanishing dune
and westerly tide

in the only photo
that I dare to keep
there you are yet where
we have come at last to meet
in the sweet summertide

the road that brings me
through a garden to your door
one thousand times
I've run this course in dreams
one thousand nights or more

brag, my Catullus,
of the sail, long in tatters,
of your little yacht
once seaworthy, indeed, but
lately beached and left to rot

the goldenrod
in the evening wind
shakes itself
free again
of a sparrow

let the moon tonight
be my faithful companion
and when morning comes
let it ride on a clear sky
brilliant moon of my desire

it is a small hill
that I climb
the showy aster
waxing coldly on
the windward side

when the swallow lands
and tucks beneath a wing
the sky of evening
you barely pause but withdraw
icily clasping your robe

long incised upon
an upright slate of stone
the now illegible
but once familiar name
of one left here alone

when my hand neglects
to turn the page, Alice,
the testy Queen,
the deck of cards—all
scatter with the autumn wind

I'm immured tonight
in my arid study with
divers brittle books
and every text I lift
exhales its share of dust

November weather
finds me well along
a familiar path
a low wind gray in the grass
and here and there a stone

his antique voice
is like that of
the wind or of
the quail before
the withered grass

let the evergreen
be so
whether in a burning sun
or in a long night
aglitter with snow

a withered garden
left again
to the care of
one piping
sparrow

when you call my name
so soothingly, I rise
and drift from that dream
and shiver to hear the tick
of sleet on the windowpane

no way to skip it
but I toss the stone
sidearm nonetheless
and listen to it clatter
across the frozen river

constant evergreen
of a winter's day,
familiar evergreen
of constant desolation —
who will visit you, come spring?

ice pulls back away
from the wind-protected,
sunny island shore
and, into that unexpected
pond, the cold, the quiet swan

Drifter

left to make
a packing box
your table
and take for your ration
in lieu of bread, air

and praying for rain in the heat of the day, for a vacant
foyer or underpass in the rain, for another packing box

like the scrap
of brown paper
lifted up
from that foul gutter
on the evening wind

you too rise
from where lately
you loitered
driven now drifting now
hither now thither

Halo

With nothing better to do, with immoderate desires but a modest income, with little more than youth to support me, I devoted my days to rummaging through dusty stacks of public lending libraries and my nights to scouring the books I'd brought home. My reading was not systematic but reflected only my capricious curiosity. History and religion, fiction and philosophy, painting and poetry were all fair game. If a title proved disappointing, I quickly set it aside without any sense of loss, without any regret for time wasted. If a book, on the other hand, captured my fancy, I devoured it by the halo of my lamp, sometimes finishing one, two or three volumes before first light.

This is how I squandered the fortune of my youth—on the luxury of reciting aloud another man's finely-tuned phrase or praising the harmony of another man's palette. Those of my peers who were more circumspect studied the mysteries of making money while I mastered the way of that labyrinth, the library. My friends came to lament the sacrifice of their liberty in acquiring fine possessions; I came to lament the poverty of my proud independence. Isn't it a simple matter, in retrospect, to say this man is illuminated, this man is not—to weigh, resolutely, wisdom against folly?

by the dark but
fragrant signature
of ink on paper
I learned the ancient graces
of what fields what flowers

there must be a book
about this place
with such counsels as
may save me from the lonely
fall of a winter's night

I sit beside
a lamp
and in the warmth
of that company
turn a page

Confessio Amantis

he picks it up and
lays it flat upon the palm
of her small hand
the leaf of the ginkgo looks
like a broom now like a fan

she takes it up and
shuts it fast within
the pages of her book
this gilded leaf that the wind
swept up then brushed aside

Open the paperback when and where you will, the scene is
constant and the declination of the light unchanged. How
familiar the setting, the characters seem. They will live
there happily ever after.

Turn the corner of a page or let a score and more flip
rapidly through your fingers. It is a black and white film
now, grainy and flickering, running skittishly through the
sprockets. The lighting is poor or the film deteriorated.
The fictive lovers could be courting in any period and any
country or, if you will, out of time and in no place at all.

Coarse Thread

There, at the fishmonger's, you are left in the cold, waiting before the frosty aura of that glass-encased selection, waiting while the white-aproned proprietor with thin moustache, who once alluded to his many amours in Lisbon, bickers in Portuguese with his dark and diminutive better-half, waiting while the good woman wraps today's fresh catch in butcher paper, tying it off with coarse thread.

>for the wounded voice
>of the old world, no
>translation's needed—
>a rainbow's perfect pout
>on a twinkling bed of ice

Their duet—now bitter, now sweet—does not flag as you trip, upon exit, the little bell above the door.

Partial Census

Oxyrhynchus

out of that venerable heap
of everyday trash, receipts
of sale, a partial census,
tax assessments, ledgers, soiled
sayings of the Son of Man

and earlier verses, too, from a daughter of Lesbos inscribed
to mourn Time's appropriation of once tender flesh, one
hundred thousand scraps of papyrus *in toto*—the lacunae
that everywhere punctuate their Coptic, Greek and Latin
offering a literal glossolalia of the dead—plus those
impeccable gentlemen Grenfell and Hunt, they and their
baggage hence translated from an Egyptian pit to the cozy
quarters of Queen's College, Oxford, the litter of a
millennium laundered, catalogued and filed

Green Apples, 1873

to tame the tempest
of youthful grandeur and
Romantic excess
let the new motif be bland—
a handful of green apples

what other
than green will do
to signify
the true temper and hue
of everlasting spring

let the apple be
what it was or is
once smuggled from
the precincts of
a hidden garden

it has the color, too,
of a hard but glorious
and dry midsummer
not for the time being sweet
but frankly firm and sour

With Camille Pissarro, at Pointoise, and with Hortense Fiquet, also, Cézanne spent that turbulent spring and burning summer after the *annus horribilis* of the Paris Commune—with the older painter and decided anarchist Pissarro as master on those *plein air* expeditions, with Hortense and his now-toddling Paul safely concealed from the prying eyes of the domineering father Louis-Auguste, moneyed milliner and banker.

Would not Papa, who did not approve of his painting, discontinue his promised monthly grace of 200 francs, just as he'd once threatened—would not Papa do so, should Hortense and little Paul be discovered?

In good weather, into the meadows then for that daylong adventure with old Pissarro and oils and brushes, and in the evenings, home to the bliss of a young mistress and son, and on the odd days when it might rain, arranged carefully on a table for the still-life study, green apples.

A Record of Semimaru

Dilapidated but inhabited: a straw-thatched hut.

Coarse-spun and tattered: the rags of the hermit.

Before the door of his hut, by the dust of the road, disheveled where seated: the same with his biwa.

He is a stranger—this one called Semimaru—but a native of this village. A beggar, some say, but of royal blood. He sees, though blind from birth, where many do not.

Chanting long forgotten poems, he tames his own tempestuous and wayward spirit. Plucking four strings with a plectrum, he quiets an autumn gale.

Here on this mountain pass, by the road to the ancient capital, only this silk-stringed instrument does not abandon him.

> the back of the biwa,
> though delicately inlaid
> with fine hammered gold,
> is wooden and shallower
> than a begging bowl

How early twilight settles now upon this litter of straw and, in branches that lately showered travelers with red and yellow, purple and tan, a chilly wind keens over a makeshift hut, a moonless evening offers no light . . . . How dark it has become—this autumn lantern!

> one comes now one goes
> one is known and one is not
> all are travelers here
> merely passersby who part
> on the road to the capital

The boxwood body of the biwa is carved with a polished curve, like that of the pear that Semimaru's want will not afford, and smooth to touch, having weathered the four seasons. The strings of silk are drawn taut, the plectrum in his knotted hand.

> this hail that begins
> well before the dawn
> hail that stops only
> to peck at the straw again
> neither hail nor biwa end

Peach Blossom Spring

Tao Qian or Tao Yuan-Ming, sixteen centuries and countless generations ago, chose the rudeness of the common country path over the sophisticated corridor of imperial preferment, the patient poverty of studious seclusion over the ready riches of a busy courtier's life. He meditated upon the suffering of the poor and the barbarity of war, scribbling, in-between cups of borrowed wine, "Peach Blossom Spring." This tale of the discovery, by a daydreaming fisherman, of a hidden sanctuary of peace and plenty, one founded by refugees who fled the world of civil strife three dynasties before the fabulist's time—how deep Tao Qian's longing goes, how it runs on forever like the winding stream, the same today and yesterday.

> letting a dory
> trace a meandering stream . . .
> a lullaby of
> lazy water immerses
> the drifter in reverie
>
> this secret hamlet
> that one enters by chance
> here, here

the peach blossoms
of Tao Qian

the village founders
fled to this green hideaway
in a time of war
and left the outer world
farther, farther behind

in a time of war
I too would flee here
peach blossoms
scatter and color
a villager's white hair

flutes and drums
and cymbals too . . .
what can one do but join
the many who pass by
in the colorful parade

one wooden waterwheel
after another turning
peaceably herein
and close by, in clear currents,
the wavering waterweed

one wooden waterwheel
and yet another . . .
the humble and white-haired
know neither want
nor the word "mine"

not yet immortal
they live on, undisturbed,
where the water
is washed clean of all
but peach blossoms

leaves gathered
for evening tea
with Tao Qian
hurrying back
to a grass hut

I too would sit
with the ancient ones
for a time
in the delicate shade
of peach blossoms

The Trial of Dorothy Talbye, 1638

Is this the City of Peace then, with a shore cold and stony enough to harbor a Puritan predisposition? Call this Salem—the wild and unexplored interior at your back, the icy brine of the sea in your hair, in your teeth.

> here comes a dour man
> in buckler and broad hat
> and black homespun
> and a woman in russet
> who flies up behind him

For the poverty of your lot, Dorothy Talbye, let Salem console you. Why must you grieve? Are you not respected for piety and embraced by your church? Are you not wife to the good man John, and has he not blessed you with children? For counsel, visit the Elders and commune with the congregation. Be not melancholy but let us pray, sister, and you shall heal by and by.

But the private revelations of God drown out a sister's comfort, a brother's advice. Your jousting with neighbors is pronounced and frequent. The Court summons you for an alleged attack upon your husband. You neglect to appear.

Questioned by the Church Elders, you affirm that God daily instructs you to starve your husband and children, daily forbids you to spare your own person.

You, Dorothy Talbye, are not quite yourself but house a spirit or several. Will you, Dorothy Talbye, banish this demon and be freed of his bonds? You will not? Then be henceforth cast from this Church.

> they are your judges
> and they are men, the Elders,
> in their fine doublets
> white ruffs and white cuffs
> righteous and portly
>
> they are your judges
> dour in bucklers and broad hats
> and black homespun
> the ones who glare from the bench
> while you rain curses upon them

You stand accused of mischief against your husband, Dorothy Talbye, and of incivilities to your neighbors, and you are summoned to this Court, and yet, good mistress, you are haughty and do not appear. You say you are directed by God but this Court says otherwise—that you be bound and chained to the post in the Commons, that you, this July in the Year of Our Lord 1638, be whipped publicly lest Pride persevere.

> how many lashes
> may the woman bear
> how many lashes
> before, good sir, all
> turn, turn to ashes?

And so you spend some weeks quietly, duly chastised and outwardly conforming, until now, in October, in a secluded grove, Difficult, your three year old daughter, is discovered cold and breathless.

Apprehended and questioned, you freely admit that your hand broke the neck of Difficult, your darling. *Was this not mercy*, you ask, *to spare the child a future misery?* Eloquence does not follow you to Court, however, where you stand "mute for a space" and will not plead. Governor Winthrop, to loosen your tongue, threatens to place you under *peine forte et dure.* You mumble at last, *Guilty*, with your world hanging by that thread, but repent you will not.

why deplore the voice
that guides your every step
and whose purpose is
to rain commands upon you?
relent God will not

To the Commons, again, where your fellow pilgrims and your gallows wait. You will not walk, Dorothy, and so you are dragged. You will not stand and so you are lifted and supported.

Will you repent then, good woman?

Nay, nay, it shall not be so.

When the hood is placed on your head, you tear the hood off. The noose is tightened about your neck—and this, too, you would remove—but the hangman is a quick one and tires of your tricks.

Even there, at the end of the rope, you try your last to steady your helter-skelter world. You swing out and back. You reach for the gallows' ladder but you pass and win from your townsmen a final gasp.

Blue Flag

Another Garden

there is that place
where one may go
and deep within a garden
peacefully abide and watch
an apple harden

or so the tale is told
that he who will may find it
hidden there beyond a wall
where the one who comes to stay
does not hear an apple fall

nor is there any day
nor is there any night
but the young leaves lately known
to murmur ever lightly
soon are quieted and stone

Blue Flag

one path down
to a faraway lake
one path up
a stony hillside
to a cozy cottage

standing there
faraway upon
the other shore
the blue flag
of a dream

looking into
clear water
the blue flag
only
looking back

no offering
but blue flag
on a far shore
no color but
that of a dream

the clear water
of the lake
the wooden door
of the cottage
faraway

Venetian Blinds

a rented room
with a single window
and seaside view
a cloud now and then
and sun at an angle

an interior
intimate
but new
her high heels click
a door clicks to

coming together
in a rented room . . .
the Venetian blinds
drawn upon a royal palm
and seaside view

the Venetian blinds
let the midday light and palm
pass through to stripe
peach and green a satin sheet
and sleeping woman too

nakedly there
before
she is clothed now
the afternoon colors
splash window and floor

the interior
intimately
ebbs away
with the click of her heels
with the tide in the bay

The Black Clock

these lips of the conch
pink enough to startle
the beholder's eyes
and handless in the background
a black clock's blank face

a crystal carafe
emptily erects itself
midway between
the forward enticing conch
and tell-nothing clock

ever so slightly
the tenderly parted lips
of the conch rosily
invite one back yet again
to the primal tidal sway

a pale china cup
perilously poses at
the table's edge
a vacancy akin
to the conch's pink crevasse

a clock without hands
with a blank nondescript face
insistently there
as if wanting now to tell
of what the dark keeps

though slightly parted
to tempt the old
and young beholder
the conch whispers neither more
nor less than the clock today

A Walking Stick

a walking stick
that some ancient cast aside
I lift it from the dust
of this derelict path
and today I make it mine

on a journey
in autumn
neither wind nor grass
point the way nor speak
of a walking stick's path

let me put this stave
and one foot now before me
let me follow
wherever
a walking stick leads

the wind of autumn
that mourns in the grass
loyal companion
of a walking stick
and of its path

a walking stick
primitively hewn
what fragrance
hitherto unknown
lingers about it

the wind of autumn
blows dust from the path
and blows dust back
holes from a walking stick too
blow away with the path

autumn wind
mournful grass
precious fragrance
of a walking stick
all shall pass

a walking stick
beside the path
this, too, I would leave
in the dust
when I pass

Behind Your Name

behind your name
I behold the very Earth
and hidden garden
now that aspect that is known
now that aspect that is not

I look and look closely
for what I do not know
behind your name . . .
from whence did you come?
where now shall you go?

behind your name
a tender continent
and firm foundation
behind your name
an Earth unknown

behind your name
a sail unfurled proudly in
an evening wind
behind your name
the longed-for landfall

why name you so
after the Earth
when there is only
a lively fire or air
behind your name

colors of the soil
separated and rinsed
in a cool rain
the Earth separated
behind your name

an island like jade
in the blue estuary
an oasis deep
in the dunes
behind your name

what consuming fire lies
behind your name?
what deluge to come?
only the bright air, the clear,
behind your name

behind your name
the Earth here and there
begins to give way
and in your namesake's place
a field of flowers

behind your name
is it not the sun
behind your name
is it not the moon
each one with its true flower

The Simple News

Woodberry Tavern

wading into thick
cigarette smoke to the beat
of a jukebox
Brubeck and all that
old school jazz

The graying proprietor and his wife, too, were seated, more often than not, with a few aging cronies—familiar enough to extend an unending tab—around one circular table, a friendly lot, and cozying up in pairs for a night of Euchre or Canasta.

High ceilings of pressed, patterned tin and a long mahogany bar with a brass rail footrest from end-to-end, the taupe walls and beveled glass liquor cabinets of another era contrasted favorably with Mr. and Mrs. Woodberry— so much so, that after only a glass or two, one might penetrate that couple's wrinkled exterior and perceive their hidden youth.

tequila straight
from the shot glass
with a little lemon
and salt for a chaser
our aqua vitae

One long and narrow room, with an entrance on Water
Street and a door at the far back, the latter opening onto a
screened wooden porch on stilts and a view of the river
some 20 feet below—this is why our little band, barely
legal, came to frequent the tavern that summer: to sit and
watch the dark currents pass under our perch, there in our
high nook and hideaway, to wake to life in that deliciously
cool air of last light and to listen, in the silent intervals, to
the bankside willows gather the wind.

a dark saying
of Hêrákleitos
is quoted
and thus translated floats
away with the river

the delicate girl
the brunette who wears
a flower in her hair
she is a bit mad perhaps
she looks like Ophelia

another round
of shot glasses stops
at our table
a chorus of mock-protest
from the girls in tight jeans

the Rokeby Venus
passionately praised
for line and color
we speak of Velásquez
as if he were of our crew

and so we drift along
pleasantly enough
no ferryman near
with his forbidding shadow
when we happily ship oars

Needles by Night

coming into Needles at the end of a blistering day via
Flagstaff by way of Gallup and before that Taos Pueblo for
breakfast and the Sangre de Cristo Range

coming into Needles on the dusty coattail of a bit of night
wind and heat lightning the sand kicking up into a dinged-
up Mustang convertible to sting a sun-burnt face

       where was that village
       and when did you pass through
       you forget the name
       but recall the sign *last stop*
       for water one hundred miles

       then a straight line for
       that one hundred miles and more
       of desert twilight
       and every hour or so the ghost
       of tumbleweed floats on the road

coming into Needles Gateway to California

coming into Needles on the sly and under cover of darkness
drunk still on the vacancy of that vivid glare some hours
earlier tracked through

coming into Needles by way of the main street 10:30 p.m. a
digital bank clock remarks for the record 112 Fahrenheit it
reports soberly

coming into Needles
only to pass through
and quickly
into the wide desert
of the night again

farther down
that desolate road
and gray and scraggly through
the halo of your high-beams
the trickster coyote

Glass Lake

the water gin-clear
and five fathoms deep
light from a sunfish
scales its way back up
the azure heights

Here, on the wooden dock that sags and lists to one side
and a ripple, I watch the light now sailing back from below,
now a spire or a spine, now a fan or a fin, now alight or
adrift in the scintillating guise of a stickpin—a damselfly.

Neighbors

This north country is a relic of a glacial advance—countless lakes and thicketed vales, everywhere a trickle with or without a proper name, an expansive past gouged by a cold that receded but never quite abandoned a claim to this land.

The early settlers raised the very stone from the fields for their first homes. Trade in timber let them barter for goods until the old growth was cleared. Many left then but still a few held on, year after year, adopting the chiseled tenacity of the stones, adapting to the quiet decorum of their resolute neighbors.

> an acre or two
> and little is sown
> in the poor soil
> but hill after hill
> stone on stone

Soberanes Point

the smooth white belly
of a washed-up shark
exposed and torn
the light of this day peels back
and ebbs away with the tide

the very rocks
that shouldered
froth and spray
loom above the water they
and their jagged shadows

ripples everywhere
in the fine sand
repeated ripples
that echo a last
wave's retreat

on the saw-like
teeth of the shark
on the gaping mouth
without smile or grimace
a little lingering light

going barefoot going ghostly over the sand after the heat of yet another brittle day the dark draws near cool and clinging in one whispered breath the Pacific's burden of brine is brooding but familiar and on the winding coast road headlights behind us now and then a beach bonfire before that undertow where no one floats a flame tended by anonymous faces smudged anonymous hands erased by that glow and by the occasional dry spittle of sparks

Pimento Walk

her cousin Blue
rattling change in his pocket
starts the jitney up
from a beach lined with palms to
a precipitous hinterland

she remembers
her mother's father now
a Maroon he was
what long hair what fiery eyes
sharpening a machete

the road is narrow
and winding higher yet by
mango and waterfall
the macadam is level
only on the mountain top

somebody's goat
nods warily
somebody's skinny daughter
sets upon her pretty head
a pail of water

Thirty to forty simple houses and one shanty-like general store lie scattered along the ridge. The Caribbean, with its diamond-like faceting, sparkles far below. *Pimenta dioica*—with a rich fragrance that recalled for the colonial British landowner cloves and ginger, cinnamon and nutmeg at once, thus winning the sobriquet *allspice*—blossoms in the wild and in the yards, remnants of what, amid the guinep and jackfruit trees, once stood as a great plantation. Out of the jitney, in the aromatic splendor of her childhood home, she remembers her grandmother's tales of her childhood in this place, of village elders born out of slavery, of a genteel Victorian mistress with airy crinoline and parasol and her gentleman beau, hat in hand, on a luxurious walk under the perfumed canopy.

Little Fig—Tanka

out of the beak
of a mourning dove
nothing less than
the new day itself
bittersweet and gray

the yellow shingle
and old-fashioned leaded panes
the weeping willows
that hide it from the river road
little shack I long for so

a plain-spoken gull
with a plain-spoken greed
nothing more
to illuminate
a deepening spring

I see the writing
on the wall
but graffiti begets
graffiti until
all is illegible

on a bright day
frightful news . . .
and if the world takes
a turn for the better?
inclement weather

the road to you
is difficult and far
and if I strive
ten thousand days and more
I will not have you while I live

it was your one gift,
this would-be diary,
and so I have left
the book as it was—bound
and blank, sans confession

I study the swan
and neither in that hissing
threat and straightened neck
nor in that glassy glide
do I find the god disguised

about your letter
to the world . . .
the simple news today
is this: nobody reads,
nobody writes

I found it hard to
swallow—the spiteful temper
and lack of reason
that cursed the little fig for
being out of season

I would have you now
delicately in indigo
and daringly sheer
for the dawn of summer,
beautiful morning glory

nothing to say
I say nothing
no one to write to
I write to no one—the voice
of a poplar leaf

one week after
the vivid fact
of fire in the grass
soot is the flower
the petals black

I put the posts and
slats up eagerly for
the privacy fence
but today I plan
to pull it down

the water is clear
at last
and so I look and see
how the current runs
from deep to shallow

the windfall apples
call the whitetail deer
to that mild ascent
where, throughout the afternoon,
the clouds sail on, sail on

the goldenrod
alone at the somber edge
of the sodden field
unsullied and erect
coldly glistens in the rain

deliciously sweet
but with a slight tang,
the rejected
and twisted little
apples of Winesburg

the moon is bright
and keeps me company here
the moon is bright now
and happily finds you where
love may not ever after

the stunted pine
that I planted years ago
still stands there
stooped over
refusing to grow

every man is vain
though the point may differ—
looks, wealth, wit . . .
you flaunt, friend, a borrowed sail
and rudderless, creaking ship

the grass is withered
and every flower
of the field also
their proud colors muted now
muddied red, gray or brown

I swept the spare room
but left its vacancy
alone, intact—one
bare light bulb, one
rectangle of black

a half-day's travel
gets me there in time
to look it over—
the cold harbor, at last light,
and rain at my window

I did not flinch but
closely weighed her every word
and only then walked out
as I'd walked in, alone,
through a withered garden

like the weight of
a great stone to
the calloused hand
now stonily numb
this winter sun

the night is cold
but it is faithful and so
I will not leave its side
but here at my window bask
in the light from the snow

I let it go
the little fury
of bright confetti
that will now be
nobody's letter

the sky is one
with the field today
and left to right
for the snowman
continuously white

someone says, let's stay
someone says, let's go
the night is black and
jaggedly cold but
there's light from the snow

TOR HOUSE

You, Jeffers, coveted a savage beauty and settled on this headland. Insisting that *man will be blotted out, the blithe earth die*, you gathered granite from the cove below, placed stone on stone, built a refuge with your hands from the vanity and violence of man's numbers, man's progress. Though you were well aware that

> *The square-limbed Roman letters*
> *Scale in the thaws, wear in the rain*

you praised this coast in poems, you loved a woman and here raised two sons, foreordained, like all flesh, to oblivion. Or so your stubborn eloquence would have it.

Before your death, you witnessed this granite perch being hedged by others' houses and lamented your loss of *an unbroken field of poppy and lupin*. Even so, these pilgrims that you living sometimes pitied, sometimes despised, they come now to marvel at your handiwork, even now to rest their hands upon your stone.

not far from the house
I find the wind-worn
Monterey cypress
did you plant this twisted one,
this gaunt one, this evergreen

I, too, regard
the red-tail hawk and watch
in the sunset where
above your sea-battered cliff
he rides the wind alone

go, then, with the grain
of this, your granite—
I see you there, a child
of the wind, of the tide . . .
and brother to a stone

Seamen's Bethel, New Bedford

> the boys would have grog
> and mealy hardtack, mother,
> and are gone a-sailin',
> the boys for grog are gone down
> to the hold with the captain

That rasping shanty of a drunken nor'easter comes and goes briefly to come, again, and rattle the panes in this chapel with stammering sleet.

I have come here—perhaps as Melville once did—for a respite from December's bitter weather. Thirty-one cenotaphs on the wall name and number the men who did not dock, again, at this port—an Icarus who fell headlong from topmast to deck, a Jonah who paled as a shark's morsel, a Joseph somehow lost by his seafaring brethren. A ship's log preserved each of their names, though their bodies it could not.

> thirty-one tablets
> of stone on the wall
> and what then? what
> then should one tablet
> happen to fall?

But in New Bedford, Melville wrote, *actual cannibals stand chatting at street corners; savages outright; many of whom yet carry on their bones unholy flesh. It makes a stranger stare.*

The Quaker merchants, too, fretted over the souls of sailors who'd snuggle up with a fifth in a local brothel and founded, after gnawing on that bone, the New Bedford Port Society for the Moral Improvement of Seamen. Hence, this salt-cured and seasick chapel.

The light of this world for a time is dipped with whalers in the blood of their prey, the flesh and harpoon together cleansed. *Ego non baptizo te in nomine patris*—how cleverly Melville put a sinner's Latin in the mouth of his mad captain!—*sed in nomine diaboli* . . . . The wick in the oil lamp gutters.

> would he send me
> a fin of that Whale
> on the devil's tines
> forged in a hail of sparks
> yet raw from snout to tail

The winter light of New England is constant and pewter on the panes. I rise to take my leave but the thirty-one tablets stay, the winding-sheet of the wind unraveling below in the harbor.

> I've sat in his pew, then,
> not unpredictably far
> back from the pulpit . . .
> I shut the chapel door, sleet
> on the cobbles of Johnny Cake Hill

Leaning Back

in the black and white
Polaroid snapshot
on a rollercoaster
ride of a gravel road
ready for anything

leaning back on the side panels of a '55 Ford Thunderbird
still sparkly still new in that north country the cool mint
blue paint the high and cloudless summer sky of a child
leaning back with the young tough in white tee shirt and
jeans the wavy-haired James Dean look-a-like and father
who is momentarily free of eking a living

out of a long gray
shift of confinement
at the tire plant
the sunny and beautiful
road going nowhere

Morro Bay

The girlfriend who doubles as her roommate, she says, came home in the early hours, by car, from her mother's place in Topanga Canyon. I sit by a window nearly as narrow as the slit of my rum-soaked eyes and stare offshore at a keep of wild rock that tilts a towering shadow like a pointer—toward how many flowering islands?—in the California spring. Her satin robe parts innocently as she tosses back her platinum pageboy with bangs and I taste the salt in the air.

> a seaworthy trawler
> called from night
> fishing to port
> rolls with a billow
> in the morning glare

Somewhere between midnight and dawn, I misplaced her name. She does not ask me and I do not tell her mine.

Notes to the Poems

Photograph at 19 (p. 22): Jack Kerouac explored Route 66 most famously in *On the Road* (New York: Viking Press, 1957).

Leon Trotsky, founder of the Red Army subsequent to the Russian Revolution of 1917, opposed the rise of Joseph Stalin after the death of Vladimir Lenin. He was expelled from the Communist Party in 1927 and deported from the Soviet Union in early 1929. He lived in exile, thereafter, in Turkey, France, Norway and Mexico. In Mexico, Trotsky was at first the guest of the famous muralist Diego Rivera and his wife, the painter Frida Kahlo, but later took up his own residence in Coyoacán where, in August 1940, a Soviet loyalist wielding an ice-pick assassinated him.

Pravda, Russian for "truth," was the official newspaper of the Central Committee of the Russian Communist Party from 1912 until its cessation in 1991.

Frida Kahlo (1907-1954) painted *Las Dos Fridas* in 1939; it is housed in the Museo de Arte Moderno of the Instituto Nacional de Bellas Artes in Mexico City.

On August 6, 1945, the B-29 Enola Gay dropped the first atomic bomb on the city of Hiroshima.

The questionable occupations of Arthur Rimbaud in Africa are the subject of Charles Nicholl's *Somebody Else: Arthur Rimbaud in Africa 1880-91* (Chicago: University of Chicago Press, 1999). The sixteen year old prodigy Rimbaud, in a letter to George Izambard on May 13, 1871, wrote "Je est un autre," that is, "I is another." In the prose poem "Vagabonds," he wrote, "J'avais en effet, en toute sincérité d'esprit, pris l'engagement de le rendre à son état primitif de fils du soleil, —et nous errions, nourris du vin des cavernes et du biscuit de la route, moi pressé de trouver le lieu et la formule," which Louise Varèse rendered, "I had, in truth, pledged myself to restore him to his primitive state of child of the Sun,—and, nourished by the wine of caverns and the biscuit of the road, we wandered, I impatient to find the place and the formula" (*Illuminations and Other Prose Poems*, Revised Edition, New York: New Directions, 1957, pp. 64-67).

Oxyrhynchus (p. 43): Bernard Pyne Grenfell and Arthur Surridge Hunt began excavations in 1896 of the various dumps that served the ancient settlement of Oxyrhynchus, Egypt. The cache of papyri that they and their successors uncovered (investigation of the sites continues to this day) has led to the publication by Oxford University of 70 volumes with a further 40 volumes planned.

Among the finds are important Greek poetic and dramatic texts by Sappho, Pindar, Sophocles and Menander, scientific and historical works by Euclid and Livy, ancient Christian fragments of known and previously unknown texts plus countless private and public documents important for the study of the political, economic and social history of ancient Greece and Egypt.

A Record of Semimaru (p. 46): The subject of this work is a blind poet and biwa player of Heian Japan. One of his waka, collected by Fujiwara no Teika (1162-1241 M.E.) in *Ogura Hyakunin Isshu* ("One Hundred Poems, One Hundred Poets"), found favor with successive editors of imperial anthologies. Contradictory legends about Semimaru were preserved in *Konjaku Monogatari* (12th century) and *Heike Monogatari* (13th century). He is also the eponymous subject of a Nō play by Zeami (15th century).

The Trial of Dorothy Talbye, 1638 (p. 51): Early common law permitted the punishment of *peine forte et dure*—the placing of heavy weights on the chest—for persons accused of a felony who refused to enter a plea. Weights were added incrementally until a plea was extracted or the accused suffocated.

The Black Clock (p. 62): "The exquisite *Still Life with Black Clock* of c. 1869-1870 is a study of intricate formal balances and masterful design: the rococo curves of the shell at left, the vertical, fluted vase at centre, the sombre black box of the clock at right all rest on the austere white slabs of the cliff-like cloth. Although the imagery suggests some intimate level of veiled meaning—the sensuous scallops and red-lipped mouth of the shell, for example, seem poised to assume more than a formal role—the work also resists our attempts to read any specific symbolic connotations into it. Even the authoritative black clock, missing its time-telling hands, refuses to act as a traditional still-life symbol." (Mary Thompkins Lewis, *Cézanne*, London: Phaidon Press Ltd., 2000, pp. 87-88).

Tor House (p. 92): From Robinson Jeffers, "To the Stone-cutters," in *Tamar & Other Poems* (1924): "Man will be blotted out . . ." and "The square-limbed Roman letters . . ."

Also, from Robinson Jeffers, "Carmel Point," in *Hungerfield & Other Poems* (1954): "an unbroken field of poppy and lupin . . . ."

Seamen's Bethel, New Bedford (p. 94): Herman Melville, *Moby-Dick*, Chapter 6: "But in New Bedford actual cannibals stand chatting at street corners . . . ."

Melville, *op. cit.*, Chapter 113: "Ego non baptizo te in nomine patris . . . ."

Melville to Nathaniel Hawthorne, June 29, 1851: "Shall I send you a fin of the Whale by way of a specimen mouthful? The tail is not yet cooked—though the hell-fire in which the whole book is broiled might not unreasonably have cooked it all ere this. This is the book's motto (the secret one),—Ego non baptiso te in nomine—but make out the rest yourself."

Lagniappe:
Two Essays, One Interview

The Road Ahead for Tanka in English

Introduction: Five Lines in Search of a Context

Contemporary tanka practice in English displays a marked tendency to combine and integrate discrete units and thereby extend and amplify its abbreviated form. This desire for a larger structure has centered itself, to date, on the elaboration in poetic composition and theory of the tanka sequence. The sketchy properties of tanka—understatement, suggestion and emphasis on what is not said as well as what is—invite such expansion (Garrison, 4-5). These evolving poetic forms approximate the schematic organization of Western stanzaic verse yet may allow or demand—though this is a matter in dispute—greater autonomy to the individual tanka than a stanza might possess in the Occident (McClintock, 23 and Kei, 193-194).

A parallel process is evident in the classical and medieval history of Japanese waka, the forerunner of English tanka, where integration of individual poems into larger cohesive works advanced roughly contemporaneously along two separate lines: adaptation to certain prose genres and incorporation in imperial anthologies.

Even after it is clear to us intellectually that we should not consider Japanese literary works in terms of our own genres, we may find it difficult emotionally to accept the fact that the same work may be called a tale (*monogatari*), a diary (*nikki*), or, significantly, a poetic collection (*kashū*). The shorter Japanese poetic units are quite simply more adhesive to fictional—or even nonfictional—strands of prose than our own discrete, autonomously conceived poems.

To a very considerable extent, then, a court poem is five lines in search of a context. But the context need not be made of prose. Collections such as the imperial anthologies show the same tendency to integration as do the diaries. The two main groups of poems in an imperial collection led the way to the practice of bringing separate poems together into a whole. The seasonal poems were arranged by a very natural temporal progression. . . . A temporal progression was also natural to the love poems, which were arranged in a pattern of a courtly love affair.

(Miner, 28)

Anthologies of English tanka observe Western convention which honors authorial identity and intent. Hence, poems in such collections are presented alphabetically or chronologically under each individual author's name. Organizing the texts of many poets temporally in seasonal or love sequences is generally shunned. Given the history and strength of the tradition, the liberties that editors of the Japanese classics demonstrated in relation to the individual waka are unlikely to find adoption. Practical issues of copyright, too, militate against the ancient mode of textual exegesis by setting a waka in a novel context.

What of prose, then? Exactly how did Japanese poets employ prose in relation to waka? Are such principles, more pertinently, applicable today as a supplementary or alternative architectonic scheme to the tanka sequence?

Preface and Poem-Tale:
The Jewel of Waka in its Prose Setting

Prose genres of the classical and medieval Japanese periods prove notoriously difficult to define as noted by Miner and others (McCullough, 6-7). For the purposes of our abbreviated discussion, the lengthy and ambitious works of romance, chronicle, diary and travel, such as *Tale of Genji*, *Tale of the Heike*, *Diary of Izumi Shikibu* or *Account of a Journey to the East*, can be largely set aside. Answers to our inquiries may be more readily found in a brief survey of those nascent forms of Japanese prose that lie closer to oral traditions: the preface or headnote (*kotobagaki*) and the poem-tale (*uta monogatari*).

Myths, folktales and anecdotes from eighth-century documents betray an earlier oral provenance and constitute Japan's oldest surviving tales. These stories are called *setsuwa*

> . . . a term translatable as "explanatory talk," "informative narration," or simply "telling." *Setsuwa* have in common brevity; an uncomplicated plot unfolded in plain, direct language; character delineation through dialogue and action rather than through description or psychological analysis; and a predilection for amusing, startling, dramatic, or marvelous subject matter.

> (McCullough, 7)

The preface and poem-tale share in the episodic nature of *setsuwa* while adding to its folk origin the early sophistication of a literate culture.

The prefatory notes that introduce waka are of two kinds. One is purely functional and expository in the narrowest sense, being concerned with providing the reader only with a factual summary of such basic information as the time and place of composition, the name of a patron, the public occasion of the writing or the set topic (*dai*) of a formal poetic gathering. A few examples from the imperial anthology *Kokinshū* will suffice: "On white chrysanthemums," "From the poetry contest held at the residence of Prince Koresada," "Composed when he had retired to a mountain village . . ." or the common and laconic entry, "Topic unknown" (Rodd, 127-128). The second type of headnote or preface opens itself to the anecdotal and expressive relation of material, subjective or objective, that interacts with the waka to follow and establishes a context that, to some degree, conditions the waka's interpretation just as the poem, in a retrospective turn, sheds new light on the preceding prose. The merely summary and factual preface holds no interest as literature, so we are concerned here solely with the latter type.

A common description of the poem-tale follows:

> The actual formal structure of *Genji* is the episode, and this concept of form is first realized in *Tales of Ise*. . . . The unique contribution of *Tales of Ise* is the dialogue of formal elements achieved in its structure by the interrelation of lyric and narrative qualities. . . . The narrative sections of *Tales of Ise* seem almost to be afterthoughts which have been displaced and put before the uta. The narrative quality of the prose style, terse and often ambiguous, seems definitely dependent upon the lyrical nature of the poetry. This relationship creates a structural tension as a binding force which arises from the episodic quality (*tampensei*) of the whole. While the episodic structure of the *Tale of Genji* appears much more extensive, it is proportional to the broad scope of

the work: the unity and completeness of the individual episode (or volume) remain inviolable.

(Harris, 22-23)

One comment above is particularly striking: the suggestion that the prose in *Tales of Ise* is like an "afterthought" to the poem. Not only in *Ise* but in many of the diary, romance and travel classics, the careful reader will perceive how frequently the waka supersedes the prose in importance. This disparity may be partially accounted for by the observation that poetry existed as an established medium long before the development of prose. It is very likely, also, that the waka preceded the prose, more often than not, in the act of composition. This elevation or enthronement of waka within prose is comparable to a jeweler's practice of choosing a proper gold or silver setting for a precious gem. To name this common early approach the lapidary style, therefore, would not be far afield.

Examples from Narihira and Saigyō

Tales of Ise provides a convenient starting place for this discussion. One of the earliest surviving poem-tales, *Ise* preserves the genre in unadulterated form. Furthermore, since it purportedly relates the many amorous adventures of the ninth-century courtier Ariwara no Narihira while showcasing many of the poet's waka, *Ise* can be usefully compared to prefatory notes by Narihira, excerpted from the poet's personal manuscript collection and incorporated in the *Kokinshū*.

The first Narihira waka is preceded in the *Kokinshū* by a prosaic and spare headnote of little intrinsic interest:

> Sent with a formal cloak to the husband of his wife's younger sister.

> when the color of
> royal purple is deepest
> it casts its glow   as
> far as I can see   over
> all the plants in the meadow

> *Kokinshū* #868 (Rodd, 298)

Little social context is discernible in Narihira's preface other than the blank statement of familial relations. The fact that the "royal purple" of the waka, however, "casts its glow" evenly "over / all the plants" implies that social discrimination of one sort or another is ameliorated by the gift of the cloak.

Compare the much expanded and poetic preface for the same poem now as presented in *Tales of Ise*:

Long ago there lived two sisters. One married a poor and common man while the other had a husband of high birth. The sister who was married to the commoner was washing her husband's Court cloak at the end of the twelfth month and shaping it with her own hands. Though she was trying to do her best, she tore the shoulder of the cloak because she was unused to such mean labors. She was at a loss for what she should do and thus fell to weeping and weeping. The man who was high born heard of this and felt that it really was too unfortunate. Thus, he picked out a truly magnificent cloak of the sixth rank and had it taken over with the poem.

Tales of Ise 41 (Harris, 80-81)

The conflict, barely legible in the *Kokinshū*, shows through clearly and poignantly in the *Ise* version where the reader, with the aid of the longer headnote, perceives the financial and class distinctions that divide two sisters and their respective husbands. While limiting, to a degree, the reader's free interpretation of the waka, the prose adds great depth to the significance of the gift of the cloak and to the consolation afforded thereby. The fine and telling anecdotal description of the wife's frustration and difficulty, over "mean labors" that she was unaccustomed to, carries much of the emotive content that is absent from the *Kokinshū* variant.

A subtle or slight change in a preface often accomplishes a pronounced shift in a waka's context. Narihira's celebrated farewell poem to a woman of Fukakusa (i.e., "Tall Grasses Village"), in which he mourns that his cultivated place will become wild and overgrown, and his anonymous lover's reply, wherein she compares her fate to that of a crying quail, are preceded in the *Kokinshū* by the flatly factual, "When he had been living in Fukakusa, Narihira sent this to someone there to tell her he was going to the capital" (Rodd, 328). The waka in question gain nothing by this exposition. Simply turn, however, to the headnote in *Tales of Ise* 123: "Long ago there lived a man. Did he not gradually become tired of a woman living in Tall Grasses Village? For he recited this poem . . ." (Harris, 155). The rhetorical question, with its emphasis on the verb "to tire," empowers Narihira's lament but truly enlivens the lady's quail against the desolate background of tangled grasses and thickets:

> if all becomes dense
> fields   I will pass my years
> crying like the quail—
> for surely you will come   if
> only for a few days' hunt

Kokinshū #972 (Rodd, 329)

The two prefatory notes are of approximately equal length, yet how tragic the atmosphere and desolate the landscape are rendered in the *Ise* version.

Another interesting comparison can be made between a preface and waka drawn from the twelfth-century monk Saigyō's private poetry collection with the presentation of the same poem in *The Tale of Saigyō*, "a biography (*denki*) written in the tradition of the poem-tale" (McKinney, 1). The term biography here must be granted considerable latitude as the intent of the narration is to frame a moving and moral tale around Saigyō's most famous poems. The life is composed, therefore, of equal parts of fact and fiction.

From Saigyō's private collection of his waka:

> At a point in time when I was feeling desolate, I heard the voice of a cricket very close to my pillow:

> > At that turning point
> > With my head for the last time
> > Pillowed in sagebrush,
> > I'd have this chirping insect
> > Still be what's closest to me.

> (LaFleur, 38)

The "turning point" of the waka denotes the death-bed of the poet, the chirping of a cricket the immediate impetus for a meditation on mutability and dissolution. Examine what liberties the anonymous author of the poet's "biography" takes with this material, however, in revising the context from that of the poet alone to the poet in public attendance at the performance of Obon rites for the dead:

> On the evening of the fifteenth day of the seventh month of the following year, the moon shone particularly bright. Seeing all the people of the capital, both high and low, gathered at the graveyards of Funaoka and Rendaino to hold services for the dead, Saigyō was deeply moved.

> > If only I could hold
> > within myself the clarity of this moon
> > to light the way
> > for those along the mountain path
> > into death.

> On seeing a crowd of people holding lights:

> > On this one night
> > in early autumn
> > the vast
> > numbers of the dead
> > are visible.

Hearing the soft chirping of autumn insects:

> When I lie down on that day
> pillowed at last under the wormwood,
> I hope I may
> have the intimate voice
> of the little cricket by me.

(McKinney, 65)

The Tale of Saigyō author not only shifts the waka from a private meditation to a religious observance in the capital but further prefaces the cricket verse with two other waka: one on the clear moon, another on autumn night. Saigyō's waka continues to contemplate death but the context, again, abandons the poet's person for the objective and communal scene of Obon. The waka's tragic implications gain focus and intensity thereby.

Examples from Shōtetsu

To weigh the potential of the fully-developed preface or poem-tale, the ninth and twelfth-century figures of Narihira and Saigyō must be left behind for an examination of the early fifteenth-century waka master and Zen monk, Shōtetsu. With this poet, only the original prefaces as presented in his personal poetry manuscript remain to posterity; there are no independent poem-tales for comparison.

That a majority of Shōtetsu's headnotes are narrowly descriptive and functional should neither surprise nor detain us. His exceptions, while rare, leap from the page as uniquely artistic and captivating documents that also possess a startlingly modern spirit.

"Beginning of Spring"

On the night of the second day of the First Month of 1450, I had a dream in which there was a votive sequence for the gods at the home of Komobe Yukimoto for which I was asked to produce the first poem, on the topic "Beginning of Spring," which I composed and then woke up. Bemused by the episode, I quickly wrote the poem down on a scrap of paper but said nothing about it to anyone. Then, in a dream on the 28th day of the Twelfth Month of 1454, Yukimoto summoned me for a votive sequence and said that the first poem, on the beginning of spring, should be just the one I had composed! So fascinated was I that the poems were identical that when I presented a votive sequence I used this "dream poem" as the first poem.

> At house after house
> they seem to be
> awaiting

the coming
of spring.
In the garden,
late at night—
doing
the morning cleaning.

(Carter, 168)

One imagines that even Coleridge, with his interrupted reverie of Xanadu, might approach Shōtetsu's little narrative with awe. The monk's matter-of-fact relation of the remarkable provenance of his waka catches our interest, quite naturally. Against that background, Shōtetsu's waka assumes a plenitude of readings, especially in the oneiric portrait of an entire neighborhood busily engaged in "spring cleaning" in the middle of the night. The waka master's aesthetic and religious convictions both play a role here in the perplexingly mysterious ambiguities of his prose and waka.

Other examples from Shōtetsu might be quoted profitably but perhaps an abridged discussion of one other brilliant preface will suffice. The untitled work in question begins with the poet's lyrical prose description of an inkwell stand in the possession of a high-ranking government bureaucrat. Shōtetsu demonstrates no lack of imagination in his beguiling delineation of the scene painted on this stand: "a place where plum blossoms floated on a stream, above which a man stood on top of a bridge, with mountains in the distance and half of the moon visible on the mountain rim" (Carter, 5). The poet invites his reader to linger with him upon the expansive landscape that unfolds before a nearby stream and recedes to the faraway mountains and, even further, to the unapproachable half-moon. As if this digression on an imaginary terrain were not sufficient, Shōtetsu proceeds to inform his patient reader not only that a Chinese poem is inscribed "next to the plum trees" but to quote the poem verbatim with its description of the man on the bridge, "walking stick in hand." The master then digresses from the Chinese poem, by a similar method of association, to his own waka with its summary of the hesitant movement of the stream and of the moon itself, for the poet hearkens back to the heavenly body fixed at the mountain rim and imagines that it cannot decide whether to rise or set. An everyday household item and human artifact, an inkwell stand, substitutes here for the grandeur of a landscape scene with a sensibility that is unique and timeless.

Conclusion: Unanswered Questions

The brief survey above sought to depict how Japanese classical and medieval poets employed prose in relation to waka. Considerations of space limited this review to discussion of the most elementary prose genres, the preface (*kotobagaki*) and poem-tale (*uta monogatari*). The wedding of prose and poetry in longer forms, such as the diary (*nikki*) or travel account (*kikō*), generally continues to revolve around the narrative episode as the basic prose unit of construction with the temporal elements of a courtship or itinerary, respectively, determining the selection and order of multiple scenes.

The rhetorical question advanced earlier in reference to prose and waka integration—"Are such principles, more pertinently, applicable today as a supplementary or alternative architectonic scheme to the tanka sequence?"— may be answered only by the practice of today's and tomorrow's poets.

This unanswered question itself poses other problematic inquiries:

- To what degree does the addition of prose limit the field of possible meanings for a given tanka?

- Is the prose invariably dependent upon or subservient to the tanka or is it not, on occasion, an equal or greater partner?

- Can exposition proper not inform the composition of a preface or poem-tale and acquire poetic value, either by the diction and rhythm of what is said or by the presence in the description of matter that resonates with the tanka?

- Are longer prose genres, such as diary or travelogue, still valid for use with tanka?

- Are Western prose genres that were unknown to classical or medieval Japanese poets adaptable for use with tanka?

- To what degree, if any, must the quality of prose with tanka differ from that of prose with haiku (haibun)?

Other questions not anticipated here are certain to follow practice. If one considers the many parallels between the history of Japanese waka and tanka in English, isn't the adoption of a prose accompaniment to tanka inevitable?

Works Cited

Carter, Steven D. *Unforgotten Dreams: Poems by the Zen Monk Shōtetsu*. New York: Columbia University Press, 1997.
Garrison, Denis M. "Dreaming Room," *Modern English Tanka*, Vol. 1, No. 3, Spring 2007.

Harris, H. Jay, Trans. *The Tales of Ise*. Rutland, VT: Tuttle Publishing, 1972.

Kei, M. "Structure and Autonomy in Tanka Sets and Sequences," *Modern English Tanka*, Vol. 2, No. 1, Autumn 2007.

LaFleur, William R. *Mirror for the Moon: A Selection of Poems by Saigyō*. New York: New Directions Books, 1978.

McClintock, Michael. "Tanka in Collage and Montage Sets: Multivalence, Duende, and Beyond," *Modern English Tanka*, Vol. 1, No. 4, Summer 2007.

McCullough, Helen. *Classical Japanese Prose: An Anthology*. Stanford, CA: Stanford University Press, 1990.

McKinney, Meredith, Trans. *The Tale of Saigyō*. Ann Arbor, MI: Michigan Papers in Japanese Studies, No. 25, Center for Japanese Studies, University of Michigan Press, 1998.

Miner, Earl. *An Introduction to Japanese Court Poetry*. Stanford, CA: Stanford University Press, 1968.

Rodd, Laurel Rasplica and Mary Catherine Henkenius, Trans. *Kokinshū: A Collection of Poems Ancient and Modern*. Boston, MA: Cheng & Tsui Company, 1996 (first edition, 1984).

THE ELEMENTS OF TANKA PROSE

Introduction: Basic Definition

The marriage of prose and waka, the forerunner of modern tanka, occurred early in the history of Japanese literature, from the 8th to 11th centuries, with rudimentary beginnings in the *Man'yōshū* and later elaboration as an art in the *Tales of Ise* and *Tale of Genji*.

One aspect of the proliferation of prose with waka forms is that practice moved far in advance of theory. Japanese criticism to this day lacks consensus on a name for this hybrid genre. The student, instead, is met with a plethora of terms that aspire to be form-specific, e.g., preface or headnote (*kotobagaki*), poem tale (*uta monogatari*), literary diary (*nikki bungaku*), travel account (*kikō*), poetic collection (*kashū*), private poetry collection (*shikashū*) and many more (Konishi, II, 256-258; Miner, 14-16).

The first problem one must address, therefore, in any discussion of tanka plus prose is terminology. While Japanese waka practice and criticism afford no precedent, the analogy of tanka with prose to the latter development of haibun does. The term haibun, when applied to a species of literary composition, commonly signifies haiku plus prose written in the "haikai spirit." It would not be mere license to replace haibun with haiku prose or haikai prose as proper nomenclature. Upon the same grounds, tanka prose becomes a reasonable term to apply to literary specimens that incorporate tanka plus prose—a circumstance which may lead one to inquire, not unreasonably, whether tanka prose also indicates prose composed in the "tanka spirit."

Fundamental Structure of Tanka Prose

Tanka prose, like haibun, combines the two modes of writing: verse and prose. Verse is metered language, that is, language measured in some fashion, whether what is counted is stress, quantity (duration), syllables, metrical feet or some other feature (Preminger, 885-890; Turco, 5). In Japanese literature, tanka and haiku established metrical norms based on syllabic count. Tanka and haiku commonly abandoned syllabic meter in 20th century Japan and the adoption of the two forms in the West has widely followed suit.

Tanka prose, then, is a hybrid of these two modes of writing and one can extrapolate from this circumstance a basic unit—one paragraph, one tanka—that fulfills, at a minimum, the expectation aroused by the name.

I observed, in an earlier paper on this subject, that the simplest forms that this basic unit of tanka prose might adopt are two. The first is the preface or headnote:

> The prefatory notes that introduce waka are of two kinds. One is purely functional and expository in the narrowest sense, being concerned with providing the reader only with a factual summary of such basic information as the time and place of composition, the name of a patron, the public occasion of the writing or the set topic. . . . The second type of headnote or preface opens itself to the anecdotal and expressive relation of material, subjective or objective, that interacts with the waka to follow and establishes a context that, to some degree, conditions the waka's interpretation just as the poem, in a retrospective turn, sheds new light on the preceding prose.

> (Woodward, 2007a, 180 -181)

The second type is the poem-tale (*uta monogatari*) or episode as Harris and McKinney make clear:

> The actual formal structure of *Genji* is the episode, and this concept of form is first realized in *Tales of Ise*. . . . While the episodic structure of the *Tale of Genji* appears

much more extensive, it is proportional to the broad scope of the work: the unity and completeness of the individual episode (or volume) remain inviolable.

(Harris, 22-23)

In uta monogatari and the Japanese poetic tradition in general the poem is always the center around which the narrative episode arises. Episodes may relate outward to each other, either temporally or thematically, but this larger structure is usually of only secondary importance.

(McKinney, 13-14)

I offered illustrations in the earlier article which were drawn from classical Japanese sources, such as *Tales of Ise* and the *Kokinshū*, from the poems of Narihira, Saigyō and Shōtetsu. I wish now, since my chief interest in this paper is English adaptation and practice of these techniques, to employ works in English for discussion.

A simple and clear example of the preface or headnote is this

> —in America these trees are called acacia, but I learned to know their yellow fluffy balls of bloom could color a whole Italian sky when a rainstorm came with the other troubles I had at the time—

sunset
between April showers
clouds
of thunder and hail
boughs of mimosa

(Reichhold, 1998a, 22)

Here Jane Reichhold, in her sequence "A Gift of Tanka," sketches a pithy introduction to her tanka, giving the reader the basic scene as well as a broad hint concerning undefined difficulties of the past. If her "troubles" were even slightly elaborated, this text would shift away from the clearly expository and rapidly approach the poem-tale or episode.

A second example—this from Karma Tenzing Wangchuk —assumes a midway point between the simple preface and the nascent narrative of the poem-tale:

Traveler's Moon

Last night I left my room in central Tucson and began a residence at the Dakshang Kagyu dharma center on the east side of town.

In fall of next year, four members of our sangha are scheduled to enter a three-year meditation retreat in northern California. I moved to the dharma center in order to make preparations.

Leaving one
temporary home
for another,
a waxing gibbous moon
my companion and guide.

(Wangchuk, 2004)

Greater detail is afforded the reader by this poet who describes a relocation and a reason for it, yet no other real action is described and so the tanka prose leans back toward the basic prefatory style, despite traces and hints of narrative.

The elementary poem-tale or episode is amply demonstrated by the following work of Gary LeBel.

Rereading Tsurayuki

It's almost midnight—tomorrow's Christmas. As I turn the pages of the *Tosa Diary* I smell the sea and feel my cold soles' impress on the shingle; I hear those ancient pines whose roots are 'splashed by waves'. The rowers pull hard as a woman intones verses for the dead amid the long, elegant robes . . . I peek in on my sleeping daughter, and then shut the door.

Like the long sloping lines
in Hiroshige's woodcuts, the rain glistens
under streetlights—
what strange coasts
our bows have touched.

(LeBel, 2008)

Though this episode falls short of one hundred words, the reader is introduced to a Christmas Eve setting where a vivid renewal of an acquaintance with the *Tosa Diary* and that work's closing lamentation for a dead child awakens in the poet a concern for his own "sleeping daughter." The actual theme is never explicitly addressed but is evoked indirectly in the allusions to the work of Ki no Tsurayuki.

Quantity and Position: Tanka in Relation to Prose

If tanka prose is a hybrid genre that joins two modes of writing (verse and prose), and if the basic unit is one paragraph of prose and one tanka (whether the form is that of exposition or narration), then it is reasonable to anticipate that variation in the number and placement of tanka in relation to the prose will have some bearing upon the specific flavor or character of the tanka prose in question.

One prose paragraph plus one tanka constitutes our basic unit as well as the order of the two modes most commonly found in contemporary tanka prose. What happens, however, if that order is inverted and the tanka precedes the prose, if the prose, that is, abandons its role of preface or headnote for one of afterword or footnote? Insofar as the literature is not particularly rich in illustrations of this variant form, I shall have to cite one of my own tanka prose pieces, with apologies to the reader:

Glass Lake

the water gin-clear
and five fathoms deep
light from a sunfish
scales its way back up
the azure heights

Here, on the wooden dock that sags and lists to one side and a ripple, I watch the light now sailing back from below, now a spire or a spine, now a fan or a fin, now alight or adrift in the scintillating guise of a stickpin, of a damselfly.

(Woodward, 2008)

The three models of tanka prose basic units quoted earlier from the work of Reichhold, Wangchuk and LeBel proceed, despite their varying degree of fidelity to the rival poles of exposition or narration, in a similar manner. The prose introduces the verse and establishes a background for a closing tanka that either veers obliquely away from the paragraph or quietly reaffirms it. In an inversion of this common order, the tanka in "Glass Lake" shoulders some of the burden that is carried by the prose in the other tanka prose pieces and establishes a backdrop as well as a tenor for the prose that—now thrust into the foreground— echoes the lyricism of the opening verse.

Tanka prose, of course, is not limited to this basic unit of paragraph plus tanka but admits many compound variations of form as well. Here is a relatively straightforward example by Jane Reichhold of an expository opening which is followed by three tanka:

> . . . Mr. Warabi was soon playing the grand piano and two young men were standing before the group singing. They were singing in English and I strained to make out the words. After a bit I recognized through the operatic runs that they were singing my tanka. I was so touched that my words could be combined with such beautiful music that tears started again. Tohru Warabi had truly created a miracle out of my small words.

> your sleeping breath
> night rain revives the earth
> waves in sea air

in bright yellow daffodils
nod to the dark wind

getting older now
the sun rises so much later
in winter's approach
yet this glorious day fills
with my thankfulness in it

almost young again
in the year of my rebirth
time passes so fast
lost in childish wonderment
snails, dandelions and sunshine

(Reichhold, 1998b)

The journal commemorates an invitation from the Emperor and Empress of Japan to attend the New Year's Poetry Party as an honored guest on January 14, 1998. The prose opening delineates the setting and cultural milieu that serve simultaneously as motive and background for the celebratory tanka that follow. The contrast between the formal, full-dress occasion in a rich interior that the prose describes and the colorful rustic simplicity of the tanka could not be more vivid. Similar examples of a prose preface to multiple tanka but with very different tonal affect can be found in the works "Perfect Fever" by Marc

Thompson (Thompson, 23) and "Peach Blossom Spring" by this author (Woodward, 2007b, 171-173).

If only to demonstrate the great flexibility of this genre, I offer, by way of contrast, a recent work from Patricia Prime with a more complex structure and one where the prefatory prose and tanka elements vie with each other to lead the way in rhythm and tropes:

Wings Over Water

at first glance

you are a butterfly in flight wings flap as you dance above the red-stained Japanese bridge ready to land on a blank page

at first glance

your head bobs from side to side like the cautious mallards on the river a thousand words and lines the tools of writing tucked into your backpack in the spring when cherry blossom petals flutter to the ground or in darkest winter when the sun disappears behind the Kamai Ranges

at first glance

you are a heron wings beat and legs tangle as you swoop
along the riverbank your eyes on the light

> a harrier hawk
> scrolls the valley
> its wings
> almost touch
> the azure ceiling

> wildflowers
> in the meadow
> you scrawl
> words across the page
> illegibly

> the cramp
> of your gnarled hand
> over the paper
> a part of yourself
> a part of the poem

> (Prime, 2008)

The episodic tanka that close this strong elegiac
composition can be read in the spirit of an envoi to the
work proper or even as an extended coda. The prose
achieves its heightened effect by various poetic devices: the
use of a refrain ("at first glance"), compression due to
omission of punctuation and of certain conjunctions and

prepositions, plus the close observation and sensory images used to depict the scene.

One common method of compounding the basic unit of prose plus tanka is by continued rotation of the two modes: verse, prose, verse. A light and witty example of this model can be seen in the following work by Bob Lucky:

Strategies

> hoping
> to get the girl
> I study the sky
> and try to untangle
> the stars

Next morning the electric lines are strung with ice. No one is going out in this. I see what I have and formulate a plan for chilequiles of sorts: an unopened jar of salsa, half a bag of tortillas chips, a hunk of dried-out cheddar, two brown eggs.

> wanting
> to get the joke
> I follow the chicken
> across the road
> to the other side

I test the eggs for freshness in a bowl of water. One floats to the top. I boil the other and make nachos with everything else. "Breakfast," she says, "for new lovers," toasting us with a darjeeling I was saving for a special occasion.

> wishing
> to know the truth
> I lie awake
> exhausting
> the possibilities

(Lucky, 110)

Forms where verse and prose alternate or are interlaced show a tendency toward close relation between the two modes. This can be clearly discerned above where the successive tanka and prose installments build upon the images immediately before them: sky, electric lines, brown eggs and the chicken "across the road."

Just as our basic unit of tanka prose can be inverted, as already discussed, compound forms admit inversion also, often with striking effect. The work of Patricia Prime, again, is exemplary in this respect:

White & Red

> *The plum blossom*
> *that I thought I would show to my man*

cannot be distinguished now
from the falling snow

Yamabe Akahito
(*Love Songs from the Man'yoshu*, Vol. 8, 1426)

early spring
the snow falls softly
on white blossoms
this evening alone—
how cold it is

a sprig of flowers
I pick to place in
an emerald vase
bends under the weight of snow
fallen in the night

a serene painting
white on white
not the red
of plums that will ripen
when we meet in autumn

I admire the flowers
the faintest tick of snow
against the window
red roses sprinkled
on a white duvet

Nightfall—I approach the house. Through the lit window I see a man in a cashmere jumper, a woman in a white evening dress with a string of pearls around her neck. Her hair the black of a raven's wing, her lips painted scarlet. They sit side by side in front of the piano, playing Mozart with two hands—their free hands around each other's waists. Discarded outer clothes in a heap beside the fire. On a table, an open bottle of red wine and two glasses . . . I stand watching these two people immersed in each other. They're friends of mine, arrived early for dinner. I'd left the door open when I went to gather the blossoms for a table piece. They've let themselves in—two people playing solely for each other.

(Prime, 2007)

The sequence of four tanka that ushers in the narrative prose here achieves a very marked, abrupt leap from verse to prose element, one that is far more oblique and disjunctive than that common to the analogous genre of haibun. That vaulting effect is perhaps more remarkable insofar as the leitmotif of color is woven so thoroughly throughout the respective verse and prose sections.

Our survey of the basic unit of tanka prose and of the many compound forms it can assume is not exhaustive but does perhaps account for those forms most commonly found. What might be called an *envelope* is yet another frequent tanka prose form: here two tanka bracket the intervening prose section or two prose sections bracket one intervening tanka section. However, I have multiplied examples already and, in the interest of abbreviation, shall move on.

Tanka Prose in Relation to Haibun Conventions: Historical Digression

Sanford Goldstein may have authored the first example of tanka prose in English with his "Tanka Walk," circa 1983, which intersperses tanka with excerpts from a diary of his exercise regimen as well as a general journal which offers the poet's reflections on life in Japan, his daily walks, his meditations upon Takuboku Ishikawa's tanka and more (Goldstein, 26-32). Jane Reichhold's *A Gift of Tanka*, a collection that is sprinkled with prefatory notes in the classical waka style, followed soon after Goldstein in 1990 (Reichhold, 1998a). Larry Kimmel's "Evening Walk," circa 1996, adopts a method akin to Goldstein's in interlacing prose, tanka, prose and tanka to document his walk (Kimmel, 1996). Assays in tanka prose multiply after this, particularly in Jane and Werner Reichhold's *Lynx* where tanka prose appears frequently in the period 1997-2003 with a gradual tapering off thereafter.

Much of this early work is executed with greater enthusiasm than finish and for understandable reasons. In 1983 or even in 1996, when Goldstein and Kimmel, for example, were attempting this hybrid, tanka was not yet widely practiced nor were there ready models in English for the would-be writer of tanka prose.

I closed my earlier article on this topic with a series of questions that were intended to identify key problem areas in the practice and theory of tanka prose. It is impractical to rehearse each of those points here, if only because definitive answers to these questions await discovery. I do wish to revisit one question of this set, however, as it has a direct bearing upon the early practice of tanka prose, viz., "To what degree, if any, must the quality of prose with tanka differ from that of prose with haiku (haibun)?" (Woodward, 2007, 187)

Examination of earlier tanka prose demonstrates the regularity with which poets of the time mixed haiku and tanka freely with the prose, often even referring to the works as haibun—a fact made clear by the editorial practice of *Lynx*, for example, where such hybrids were published under the heading "haibun," there being no separate category for tanka prose. One early practitioner—and a skilled one—who consistently blends haiku and tanka with her prose is Linda Jeannette Ward:

Island Sunrise

Awakened by the staccato calls of boat-tailed grackles, I find them strutting along the deck of our cottage, beaks pointed skyward, ebony feathers iridescent in the rays of the rising sun: a great orange ball they seem to balance in turn until a wide swath of sunbeams sparkles to the ocean horizon with an arousing brightness . . .

> on pointed beaks
> nudged higher and higher
> the morning sun

My mind pleasantly suspended in the sun's dazzling glare, the open *Tao Te Ching* lies forgotten on my lap, waiting for the restless time that is gone now . . . there's only this beach, this sky and a scattering of gulls when I return my gaze to the words before me . . .

> how delicately
> she brushes
> ancient calligraphy
> . . . yellow damselfly
> upon the *Tao Te Ching*

(Ward, 54)

Here, one recognizes our basic unit of tanka prose in compound form—doubled, as it were—but with haiku in lieu of tanka in the first unit. That the prose in "Island

Sunrise" would be quite at home in many contemporary haibun—right down to the ready resort to ellipses in prose and verse—strikes me as a fair observation.

Is the 'haibun-like' aura of Ward's work, however, due to the presence of a single haiku? Does it reflect some stylistic predilection on the poet's part? Or is it simply the product of a skilled poet who, perhaps, is also well-read in haibun? I doubt that a confident answer to any of these questions can be advanced.

Perhaps one might cautiously generalize and state that the quality of the prose in tanka prose will tend to approximate that of haibun wherever the basic unit of one paragraph, one tanka is employed alone or wherever, as in Ward, haiku is joined to the prose along with tanka. One "might cautiously generalize," and I have, but without any firm confidence in the opinion. I have done so only to indicate, by way of example, how uncertain definition is in this endeavor, even on a question as apparently straightforward and simple as the one currently under examination.

Summary and Conclusion

I offered, in the introduction above, some description of the terminological confusion that surrounds tanka plus prose, both in Japan and abroad, and proposed the simple descriptive term tanka prose as easy nomenclature for the genre.

The structure of tanka prose was defined, first, by observing that the genre weds the two modes of writing (verse and prose) and, second, that our subject in its many specific forms is built upon one common basic unit of composition (one paragraph, one tanka). It was then remarked that classical Japanese practice knew two basic forms of tanka prose—preface (exposition) and poem tale (episodic narration)—and samples of these forms drawn from tanka prose in English were provided.

Discussion then followed, at some length, of the variation in the number and placement of tanka in relation to the prose and of what effect such variation has upon the specific flavor or character of the tanka prose in question. Illustrations of the basic unit and its inversion (tanka first, prose later) plus that of many compound forms were studied and compared.

A general and abbreviated historical overview of early hybrids that employ tanka and haiku with prose closed this argument and afforded the reader some insight into the difficulty of establishing any clear and strict demarcation between tanka prose and haibun.

The common critical dictum is that practice precedes theory, a rule that I see little profit in disputing. Essays like the current one, at best, can only summarize the existing literature and extrapolate, cautiously, upon observations made while doing so. My interest in the matter of tanka prose is not strictly scholarly, at all events, but owes greater sympathy to poets and poetry, to the wish to see tanka prose widely adopted and practiced and to realize, thereby, the enrichment of tanka today and tomorrow.

Works Cited

Goldstein, Sanford. "Tanka Walk" in *Northeast* III:15, Summer 1983.

Harris, H. Jay, Trans. *The Tales of Ise*. Rutland, VT: Tuttle Publishing, 1972

Kimmel, Larry. "Evening Walk" in *Point Judith Light*, Spring-Summer 1996.

Konishi, Jin'ichi. *A History of Japanese Literature* (in two volumes) with Earl Miner, Editor, and Aileen Gatten, Translator. Princeton, NJ: Princeton University Press, 1986.

LeBel, Gary. "Rereading Tsurayuki" in *Haibun Today*, February 6, 2008.

Lucky, Bob. "Strategies" in *Modern English Tanka*, V2, N3 Spring 2008.

McKinney, Meredith, Trans. *The Tale of Saigyō*. Ann Arbor, MI: Michigan Papers in Japanese Studies, No. 25, Center for Japanese Studies, University of Michigan Press, 1998.

Miner, Earl. *Japanese Poetic Diaries*. Berkeley and Los Angeles: University of California Press, 1969.

Preminger, Alex, Editor. "Verse and Prose" in *Princeton Encyclophedia of Poetry and Poetics: Enlarged Edition*. Princeton, NJ: Princeton University Press, 1974.

Prime, Patricia. "White & Red" in *Haibun Today*, December 27, 2007.

Prime, Patricia. "Wings Over Water" in *Contemporary Haibun Online*, V4, N1, March 2008.

Reichhold, Jane & Werner. *In the Presence: Tanka*. Gualala, CA: AHA Books, 1998a.

Reichhold, Jane & Werner. *Invitation*. Gualala, CA: AHA Books, 1998b.

Thompson, Marc. "Perfect Fever" in *Lynx* XIV:1, January 1999.

Turco, Lewis. *The New Book of Forms: A Handbook of Poetics*. Hanover and London: University Press of New England, 1986.

Wangchuk, Karma Tenzing. "Traveler's Moon" in *Lynx* XIX:3, October 2004.

Ward, Linda Jeannette. "Merchants Millpond" in *Lynx* XIV:3, October 1999.

Woodward, Jeffrey. "Glass Lake" in *Lynx* XXIII:1, February 2008.

Woodward, Jeffrey. "The Road Ahead for Tanka in English" in *Modern English Tanka* V2, N2, Winter 2007a.

Woodward, Jeffrey. "Peach Blossom Spring" in *Modern English Tanka* V2, N2, Winter 2007b.

Tanka Prose, Tanka Tradition:
An Interview with Jeffrey Woodward

by Claire Everett

Jeffrey, as a preface to our interview, I want to mention how, in the inaugural issue of Modern Haibun and Tanka Prose *(Summer 2009), you described, in your editorial, how writers and readers of mixed prose and verse genres often find themselves at a crossroads where they might feel inclined to reflect on the road that led there and the many possible routes that lie ahead. I am hoping this interview will provide an opportunity for you to assist us in doing just that. It also struck me that the following tanka excerpted from your own tanka prose piece "A Record of Semimaru" seems particularly pertinent:*

> *one comes now one goes*
> *one is known and one is not*
> *all are travelers here*
> *merely passersby who part*
> *on the road to the capital* [1]

Tanka, from the eighth century *Manyōshū* until this day, have often been elicited by other tanka. Your poem, Claire, is an invitation to others to respond. This dialogue in verse can engage two contemporaries or it can reach back in time and link today's poet with one long dead. My tanka that you've so kindly quoted is an example of the latter conversation; it is, in fact, a variation upon Semimaru's poem, preserved as #10 in the thirteenth century anthology *Ogura Hyakunin Isshu* (100 Poems 100 Poets):

> coming from
> or going to
> the capital
> friends and strangers
> meet and part

Semimaru's theme is one of universal mutability or transience. Acquaintances and strangers alike, on their way to or from the capital, meet only to part. I am here today and gone tomorrow. That all is in flux is Semimaru's existential certainty; one might say, in fact, that change *is* his capital. I felt a particular kinship with this tanka and with its depiction of the material absence of any reliable or permanent center. The stability of Semimaru's capital, in the end, is illusory and, in that respect, shares the dubious character of our vain and bustling modern ones.

As editor of Haibun Today, *you are doing much to promote the reading and practice of tanka prose. With journals such as* Lynx *and* Atlas Poetica *publishing tanka prose, more and more readers and writers are being drawn to the "adventure and promise of a new world." Jeffrey, could you begin by telling us how and when you first became interested in tanka prose?*

I was drawn to tanka prose initially as a a practical matter. I wrote haibun and, in my efforts to press the prose half of that equation closer to poetry and farther from journalism, I felt in longer compositions that the sketchy, fragmentary nature of haiku was a liability. I wrote tanka also. Tanka, in my view, has greater definition than haiku as a form; it was logical, if not inevitable, to turn there for a solution.

My interest in tanka prose as a reader precedes this affinity for tanka as a practising poet. I'd studied examples of Japanese tanka prose, particularly from the Heian Period, on various occasions in the years preceding this—Ki no Tsurayuki's *Tosa Diary* and the *Izumi Shikibu Diary* in the Earl Miner translations; *Tales of Ise*, the anonymous *An Account of a Journey to the East* and Nun Abutsu's *Journal of the Sixteenth Night Moon* in their Helen Craig McCullough versions. Those few titles are a fair sampling, respectively, of tanka prose's incarnations as diary, memoir, poem tale and travelogue. Tanka prose, as I was to learn subsequently, offers much more.

In its rudimentary form, tanka prose served as a contextual frame for the accompanying waka, taking the form of a preface (kotobagaki) or poem tale (uta monogatari). In The Tanka Prose Anthology *(Modern English Tanka Press, 2008), you describe the prose of this stage in the history of Japanese literature as being "rarely more than a handmaiden to the poem." [2] Perhaps you could elaborate on this and explain how these prose accompaniments evolved over time?*

A description of early prefaces and poem tales as humble framing devices for tanka is a fair generalization, Claire. Sophisticated exceptions to that rule, nonetheless, can be read in the eighth century *Manyōshū*.

Many prefaces or *kotobagaki* are entirely functional and limited to a cursory description of the tanka's occasion or topic. Look at the *Kokinshū*,[3] for example, where the occasion of tanka 325's composition is perfunctorily recorded as "Composed while stopping for the night on a journey to the Nara capital" while tanka 257's occasion is a social event—"From the poetry contest held at the residence of Prince Koresada." The prefaces in the *Kokinshū*, often enough, blandly document the conventional topic of the poem: for tanka 336, "On plum blossoms in the snow," or for tanka 339, "On the year's end."

Sometimes greater context is provided, as in the *kotobagaki* to tanka 589:

Tsurayuki sent this letter in the Third Month, when he heard that someone else was visiting and writing to a woman he had known:

> my heart is not like
> the dew which settles on the
> flowers   unconcerned—
> each time you bend before the
> wind   my torment increases [4]

Here, the reader is provided with the season ("Third Month") and circumstance ("someone else was visiting . . . a woman he had known") that inspired Tsurayuki's tanka; he, furthermore, discovers that the poet's theme is one of naked jealousy. This is nascent narrative, the rudimentary elements for a tale. Even so, the primary purpose of this preface is to explain to the reader the why-and-wherefore of the excellent poem's composition.

Compare the Tsurayuki *kotobagaki* to Masaoka Shiki's preface to a tanka sequence written in 1902:

> Nothing is tastier than horsetails, and nothing is more delightful than gathering them. Hekigoto, who went to Akabane Village on an excursion, brought some back. When he told me he was going there again, a mood came over me to make the following tanka, imagining the scene of horsetail-gathering. [5]

The ten tanka that follow Shiki's prose focus upon scenes of horsetail ferns neglected in the fields, of horsetails beside railroad tracks, of recollections of Shiki's pastoral youth and participation in sessions of horsetail-gathering. These are poems of delight in a countryside that the poet, confined to his sickbed and facing imminent death, is now barred from visiting:

> those horsetail plants
> I once picked in the fields
> by my home—
> this I now recall
> in an alien land [6]

Shiki's prose is richer in mood and nuance than the preface I cited to the Tsurayuki poem. However, Shiki's preface does share, in common with the examples above, the transitional declarative statement that links prose to verse— "a mood came over me to make the following tanka . . . ." Greater unity of purpose between prose and verse, of course, can be established by the conscious suppression of these expository connectives that, in one sense, are the trademark of much Japanese tanka prose from the *Manyōshū* to modern times, these insistent reminders that a poem was written *because* of this circumstance or that occasion. The reader, in fact, might be left safely to infer as much by the presence of the tanka after the prose. Modern tanka prose in English, therefore, stubbornly eschews such explanatory links and chooses, instead, to blend prose and tanka closely into a harmonious whole.

Following Ki no Tsurayuki's Tosa Diary *and the anonymous* Tales of Ise, *I believe Japanese prose and waka went through an astonishing metamorphosis, flourishing in a wide variety of new contexts, for instance diary, biography and military chronicle?*

A rough idea of the extent of this dramatic proliferation of works that combine prose and tanka can be had by a simple enumeration of the classifications that medieval Japanese literary scholars devised to account for its diversity: diary (*nikki*), biography (*denki*), travelogue (*kiko*) and preface (*kotobagaki*). A tale is a *monogatari* but distinctions are made with respect to the kind of tale: poem (*uta*), romance (*tsukuri*), historical tale (*rekishi*) and military chronicle (*gunki*).

Boundaries between the various types of early Japanese prosimetrum, or mixed prose-plus-verse writing, are quite blurred as observed by such influential scholars as Jin'ichi Konishi and Earl Miner; one and the same composition may be termed variously a tale (*monogatari*), diary (*nikki*) or poetry collection (*shū*). The scholarly taxonomist can distinguish further, in those writings classed as *nikki*, between the diary with dated entries and the memoir with its freer treatment of chronology.

One possible reason no single term was employed for prose-plus-tanka writings is this: from the close of the *Manyō* period until the rise of renga, waka, our modern tanka, so dominated the Japanese literary landscape that little else was considered worthy of the name poetry. Critical attention, therefore, was not focused upon the verse-type employed with prose, since this verse was invariably waka, but was directed instead toward the narrative or expository model of the prose—tale, memoir, history and so forth. It is only much later, with the rise of haikai no renga and of its offspring haibun, that distinctions between verse-types become necessary in examples of Japanese prosimetrum.

What part did Murasaki Shikibu's Tale of Genji *play in the development of tanka prose as a powerful medium that not only established context for the poem, but served to elucidate it to the point that it was no longer subservient to the poem and indeed, that tanka and prose were capable of reciprocal enhancement?*

The early elevation of verse or later hegemony of prose are two extremes of the tanka prose spectrum. Murasaki Shikibu's *Genji monogatari* (circa 1008), one might argue, represents the culmination of the latter development. In *Genji*, the precise descriptions, absorbing characters and animated style of Murasaki's prose threaten to reduce the accompanying tanka to the incidental role of a lyrical aside.

Murasaki Shikibu, however, is not only the author of *Genji*. Richard Bowring translated and collected under one cover both her memoir and her annotated poetry collection as *Murasaki Shikibu: Her Diary and Poetic Memoirs*. The *shū* consists of 120 plus waka, each preceded by a *kotobagaki*, and these prefaces range from the merely serviceable or expository sentence to a highly poetic and suggestive wedding of prose and waka that resembles modern English practice. Look, for example, at entry 46, an ekphrastic work on the subject of a painting:

> Two or three women had opened up a side door and were sitting there viewing the pear blossom. Everyone else had fallen asleep, but one old woman had her chin in her hands and was gazing intently at the scene.
>
> > Hidden in the darkness
> > Of a spring night
> > It has no color,
> > An aged heart
> > Intent on the fragrance.[7]

Murasaki's *nikki*, by way of contrast, stands closer to the triumph of prose as exemplified by *Genji monogatari* than to the general celebration of waka that is demonstrated in her *shū*. The memoir, in fact, balances lengthy prose passages of exacting description of court costume and court ceremony with digressions that display Murasaki's acute psychological insight. Where do the waka lie in all of this? There are precious few of them (less than twenty, I believe) and they generally function in one of two capacities, either as formal praise for ranking members of the court or, where two waka are joined, as poetic exchanges between court ladies or between the same ladies and their suitors.

Jeffrey, I'd like to talk now about the variety of forms which modern tanka prose may take. How does the basic unit of one paragraph and one tanka differ from its inverted form of one tanka, one paragraph?

When the paragraph leads, the closing tanka caps the prose, Claire, and is the culminating point of the composition, a sign of the work's fulfillment. Placement of the tanka first and paragraph last disrupts our common expectation. In this inversion, the tanka may possess narrative or expository qualities that we ordinarily associate with prose, whereas the paragraph that now concludes the composition acquires, to some degree, the climactic characteristics that we customarily ascribe to tanka. Consider, for example, Dru Philippou's "Sloughing Off":

> what blooms
> and bones she keeps
> they are props
> that she will paint
> with her mountain

I would walk to Cerro Pedernal and see myself bounding up the flat-topped butte in no time. At the top, where Georgia O'Keeffe's ashes were scattered, I could race along the narrow ridge with the wind's warm handclasp and plunge headlong into the blue, sloughing off my skin among pink hollyhocks, to return home as a stranger.[8]

The concord of flowers and bones in the tanka, of rejuvenation and death, has many precedents in lyrical poetry; such material, too, is in keeping with the painting of Georgia O'Keefe, the composition's nominal inspiration. But the tanka, when all is said and done, serves as the necessary backstory for the fantasy flight, if you will, of the paragraph it precedes. The poetic core of Philippou's piece can be found in the closing sentence, in the narrator's acceptance of the "wind's warm handclasp" for her resolute descent, a leap that is meant to secure her "return home as a stranger."

With reference to the response poems and tanka pairings exhibited in the Manyōshū *period and the popularity in recent years of tanka sequences in English, what distinct features does tanka prose have over sequences?*

The presence of prose—so pliable, so receptive to sudden variations in tempo or style—distinguishes tanka prose from tanka sequences. The contrast of the two modes of writing, prose and verse, is not available to the tanka sequence by definition, and while the sequence is as capable as tanka prose of marked shifts in pace from tanka to tanka, the sequence cannot offer the immediate and dramatic counterpoint of prose and verse rhythms. Tanka prose, too, often incorporates tanka sets or sequences within its broader frame.

In other respects, the tanka sequence and tanka prose have much in common. Both value understatement and ambiguity by design; both have a penchant for episodic development, for leaping over superfluous matter and lingering upon essential detail. Both stem from the same Japanese root, the waka or tanka that first came to maturity in the *Manyōshū*.

In your essay "Prose and Verse in Tandem," you propose that verse sequences within prose are more prevalent in tanka prose pieces than in examples of haibun and you attribute this less to prescribed traditions within English language tanka and haibun circles and more to ancient Japanese tanka traditions and the very nature of tanka itself. [9] *Could you elaborate on this?*

Tanka, as early as the seventh and eighth centuries, were exchanged. Custom required that the recipient of a tanka respond in kind. A reply often echoed the original gift by borrowing freely from its language and imagery; such repetition drew the call and response poems together in an act of intimate association. These poetic pairings, in the *Manyōshū* and later imperial anthologies, illustrate tanka's native affinity for integration, for the construction of sequences of two or more poems. Consider the deliberate reiteration in this example, an exchange between the Mother of Michitsuna, author of "The Gossamer Journal" (*Kagerō nikki*), and Lady Tokihime, where the "water oats" are the court ladies who mutually lament their neglect by the "reapers," their husbands:

> Where might be the swamp
> in which they can put down roots—
> those water oats
> the reapers have harvested,
> cutting to the very bottom?

soko ni sae / **karu to** iu naru / **makomogusa** / ika naru **sawa** ni / **ne o todomu**ramu

> The marsh from which
> the water oats have vanished
> is this one at Yodo:
> people said they had struck root
> in the bottom where you dwell.

makomogusa / **karu to** wa yodo no / **sawa** nare ya / **ne o todomu** chō / **sawa** wa **soko** to ka [10]

The influence of tanka's traditions upon tanka prose can be discerned most clearly in a reading of the Japanese *chōka*, the long poem of the *Manyō* period. The body of the *chōka* consists of alternating lines of five and seven syllables but, from the time of Hitomaro on, the *chōka* was completed by a *hanka*—an envoy of one, two or several tanka. *Hanka* means "verse that repeats" and that is precisely what the tanka in this poetic appendix do; they recapitulate and amplify the *chōka's* main motifs. Each tanka in the envoy is related not only to the parent poem, the *chōka*, but to its siblings also. These relationships prefigure how the individual tanka of a sequence within a larger tanka prose composition adhere to the prose body as well as to the other members of their tanka set.

Yamabe no Akahito, in a *chōka* that commemorates an imperial outing, devotes fifteen verses to a vivid depiction of an elemental seascape and the rustic seaweed-harvesters who inhabit it. His *hanka* is composed of two tanka that recall the sweeping tide, the "gemlike weeds" and a near island:

> When the tide comes in
> And the gemlike weeds on the rocks
> Of this island coast
> Hide themselves slowly in the waves,
> Will our thoughts go after them?

When the tide pours in
Across the flats of Waka Bay
The seastrand vanishes,
And the cranes with raucous cries
Fly off to shelter in the reeds. [11]

A simple glance at the romaji transcription of the original will reveal how the reiteration of key words closely links the main poem to the envoy and the two tanka to one another. "Oki tsu shima," "shio," "tamamo," "michi"—they strike repeatedly with force, like the waves against the rocks.

Contemporary tanka prose shares this propensity for employing verses in sequence, whether at the beginning, middle or end of the compositional design. A modern example of tanka prose that parallels the *chōka's* incorporation of a formal envoy with repeated elements can be found in Michael McClintock's "Before Croissants and Coffee":

Briefly, before the morning commute, before the bakery set out its morning bread to cool on the racks, before the postman's alarm rang beside his bed, and the dog scratched, wanting out, a summer rain fell on the streets and boulevards of Paris.

You slept—I saw a dream tiptoe upon your brow and would not wake you. I watched alone on the balcony the wet, shining pavements mirror the clouds.

From below,
I hear the bread racked
and readied;
across the way a dog
trots from its door.

The postman's van
speeds by in needful haste:
the rain has ceased,
you awake,
and we embrace. [12]

Bread, postman, dog and rain rebound and echo from prose to tanka, from tanka to prose.

Again, in "Prose and Verse in Tandem," you point out the prevalence of multiple tanka and tanka sequences within tanka prose. While journals such as Modern English Tanka *and* Atlas Poetica *consistently published such examples of tanka prose, Jeffrey, other journals appeared to be more reticent. It has been suggested that the inclusion of multiple tanka was not always balanced by the "brevity and lightness" of the prose. Do you think these possible criticisms are warranted and that if this was the perception of some editors might it have limited the number of venues receptive to tanka prose of this type?*

The tanka and prose elements should balance harmoniously, whether the composition offers one paragraph and one tanka or the complexities of many tanka and many paragraphs. The demand for unity and for subordination of the parts to the whole, however, is not a problem unique to tanka prose; it is an aesthetic consideration, on a smaller scale, of the single tanka and it is a concern of the sonnet and novel as well. Where this balance is wanting, Claire, criticism is justified and I, too, am sensitive to such shortcomings in execution or conception.

You alluded to the possible reservations of various journals with respect to tanka prose. Tanka periodicals, such as *Eucalypt*, *Red Lights*, *Ribbons* and *Gusts*, are often small format, print-only publications. The mundane practical consideration of space limitations, in such venues, may work against an editor's possible acceptance of tanka prose.

There is also the question of the novelty of this enterprise in English-language practice. Early examples of tanka prose can be found in the 80s and 90s but publication of the same occurred only sporadically. Nor can it be said that much of this early writing commends itself to today's reader; it demonstrates scant cognizance of tanka prose in its classical and medieval Japanese context and therefore the English "translation" loses much. The existence of tanka prose in English was virtually subterranean until its emergence upon a firm footing in 2007; it flew "under the radar" and was invisible not only to many tanka editors but to most practicing tanka poets.

Tanka prose, nevertheless, has an ancient provenance within the tanka genre; it has been present, in one form or another, from the *Manyōshū* until the present. So the appearance of newness is only that—an appearance. Tanka prose is deeply embedded in tanka's history and shares its aesthetic. The tanka community, therefore, is not without obligation to support tanka prose and neglects it only at its own peril—squandering, thereby, a rich portion of its own inheritance.

In your essay "The Elements of Tanka Prose," the question was posed, does tanka prose suggest prose that is composed in the 'spirit of tanka?' [13] From my reading, I have seen the rich diversity of this genre and how the number of tanka and their placement within the piece can influence the overall character and flavour of the prose. For example, in one of your own compositions, "Glass Lake," the opening tanka takes on the role the accompanying prose might often carry, providing a backdrop for the lyrical prose that follows. In many of Patricia Prime's pieces, such as "Wings over Water," we see the use of refrain, the suppression of punctuation and the heightening of lyricism. As tanka poetry has evolved and we have seen the adoption of more minimalist and experimental forms, such as gogyoshi, do you think it is fair to say that the 'spirit of tanka' has acquired an air of 'anything goes?'

Two temptations beset tanka. The first lies in an appeal to ossified "tradition," in a misinterpretation or falsification of tanka that aims at slavish imitation of Japanese models in subject and form. True tradition, it seems to me, can be deciphered only by serious study of tanka literature and history, by the identification of those vital qualities that transcend generational change as well as by an identification, on the negative side, of capricious trends and stylistic mannerisms. The second temptation arises from a rejection of true tradition as an impediment to artistic freedom and the consequent abandonment of tanka form and aesthetic—license, in other words, or the attitude that "anything goes."

Sanford Goldstein, in his essay "Not Again! Tanka Strings and Sequences," lamented: "The world of tanka is extending beyond its clear definitions . . . . The tendency is to create new worlds in place of an older, more stable order, an increasingly complex world that seems to go along with the complications of modernity. This diffusion includes the writing of . . . short prose pieces with tanka . . . . And so the wayward tanka world continues." [14]

Now, I respect Goldstein's work as both tanka poet and translator but his characterization of tanka prose as a modern "diffusion" of an "older, more stable order" and as a reflection of "the wayward tanka world" is curious, if you will forgive my understatement, and flies demonstrably in the face of tanka's history. Sanford did not invent tanka prose when he published his "Tanka Walk" in 1983 nor did

I invent tanka prose when I published my essay "The Road Ahead for Tanka in English" in 2007. Tanka prose is as old—or nearly so—as tanka itself.

Look at the *Manyōshū* only. You will discover numerous examples of eighth century tanka prose sprinkled throughout its pages. One work by Ōtomo no Tabito should be singled out here as an example of the sophistication and artistry of this early tanka prose; it is entitled "An Excursion to Matsura River" and can be readily found in translations of the *Manyōshū* by Edwin A. Cranston, Ian Hideo Levy and the Nippon Gakujutsu Shinkokai or Japanese Classics Translation Committee. [15] I would like to encourage tanka poets and editors to study it. Tabito's "Excursion" opens with a prose preface that richly describes the chance meeting on the river of an elderly first-person narrator and some provincial maidens; he is so taken by their beauty that he inquires if they are not "immortals," but they, in reply, insist that they are nothing more than "the daughters of fishermen." Allusions to classical Chinese poetry are woven into the flirtatious repartee that completes the prose section. Eleven tanka follow; the first eight continue the dialogue between the narrator and young women that was initiated by the prose preface while a final set of three tanka, in an objective voice, repeats and dwells upon the main motifs of the composition as a whole. Prose and tanka are fully integrated by the many variations played upon the erotic undercurrent of such images as the delicate gem-like fish, the froth of the rapids on the rocks and the wet skirts of the maidens.

In your interview with Ray Rasmussen, "Terra Incognita: The World of Haibun and Tanka Prose," you say "every form has its own tradition, its own set of conventions, and with application, a form and attendant conventions can be learned."[16] Would you say this is true of tanka prose, Jeffrey, or is the genre still—and perhaps destined to remain—in a state of flux?

Tanka prose is one species of prosimetrum; it combines, like other members of that genus, the two modes of writing, prose and verse, but can be distinguished from its fellows by a preference for tanka as its verse component. Tanka prose is constructed upon a building block or basic unit—one paragraph, one tanka—and admits greater complication in structure through compounding of either one or both of these elements. Variation in the number and placement of tanka in relation to the prose is the prime source of its rich formal diversity. That, in brief, is a simple definition of the *form* of tanka prose.

Broadly speaking, recall that our subject, like the tanka sequence, is a member of the tanka family and therefore operates within the traditions and conventions of that genre as adapted by the English-language tanka community from Japanese models. Some Japanese conventions are applicable to English practice and some are not. Some conventions, too, are victims of history and face extinction due to changes in taste or to the natural evolution of a literary form. A relevant example of this latter circumstance can be cited from the historical development of tanka prose. Common to tanka prose of the classical Japanese period is reliance upon stock explanatory phrases to signal a transition from prose to tanka: "Thus she composed this poem," "He wrote a letter with the following," or "She replied."

Consider this extract from *The Tale of Saigyō* as translated by Meredith McKinney:

> Day and night in his thatched hut he longed for the Buddha's coming. But old friends who did not share his feeling came to see the cherry blossoms, and their talk of old times disturbed his peace of mind. Annoyed, he wrote:

> > It is
> > the one sad sin
> > of the cherry blossom
> > that people come in such crowds
> > to see it. [17]

Here, "Annoyed, he wrote" is a pointer that directs the reader from paragraph to tanka; one can omit this marker without any loss to the total composition and, from the late Heian period forward, poets increasingly do so, abandoning a convention that dominated the earlier tanka prose of the *Manyōshū* and *Tales of Ise*. This suppression of the transitional phrase is the norm in modern English practice. Look at Bob Lucky's "Three":

> In the village the church bell intones the hour. We arrive just in time to hear the monotonous clanging of noon noon noon noon—like a dotted line dividing morning from the rest of the day. After a long and leisurely lunch, we check into a *pensione* and go out to explore. The clock strikes three three three. It is inexplicably sad, like a dirge: three three three. Stopping in a café, we have a brandy we don't need, and then several espressos, as we stare at the remainder of the afternoon.

> around the steeple
> the clamor of bats
> gathering dusk
> when I touch you
> you look at your watch [18]

Lucky's work, I believe, shows us how the absence of an overt transitional phrase reflects the tendency, common to modern English practice, of seamless integration of prose and tanka.

In "The Road Ahead for Tanka in English," you describe how early examples of tanka prose in Japanese literature saw the waka enshrined within the prose, an approach which you called the 'lapidary style.' [19] *Do you think in modern English tanka prose the tanka should be capable of autonomy, or with the prose, should it merely serve to contribute to the aesthetic whole?*

I'm not unduly concerned about prescribing rules for either compositional element—paragraph or tanka. I strive, instead, to identify and isolate the exemplary tanka prose work for an intimate study of how writing's two modes relate to one another therein. Poetry precedes criticism and, if rules are wanted, prudence requires us to derive our guidelines from an empirical analysis of the best writing that the genre has to offer.

Descriptively, some writers begin with a pre-existing tanka and write prose to its order; some writers compose tanka and prose in one sitting. Some tanka, if extracted from a tanka prose work, might be capable of a meaningful and independent existence; some tanka might not.

Can't we say much the same, however, of the individual tanka that comprise a tanka sequence? Does the reader dwell, in reading the same, on the excellence of one tanka alone? Or is the reader's attention directed by the orchestration of several tanka working in concert toward one end? If the reader, upon finishing the work, is satisfied by the poetic object, is the value of the sequence diminished by a judgment that one tanka can boast of autonomy while another remains a servant to context?

In connection with the previous question, Denis M. Garrison described the 'dreaming room' quality of multivalent tanka, i.e., the "empty space inside the poem which the reader can fill with his personal experience, from his unique social context." [20] Jeffrey, do you think the inclusion of prose impinges on the 'dreaming room' quality of the tanka within a tanka prose piece, or, conversely, does the tanka devalue the prose?

I view the contemporary example of tanka prose in English as a complete poem in its own right and therefore do not distinguish between *this* tanka and *that* prose. I do not set the two modes of writing at odds. If Garrison's concept of 'dreaming room' is applicable to our subject, neither paragraph nor tanka can lay exclusive claim to it.

The prose and tanka of a single composition, Claire, mutually influence one another. Many poets write prose "around" a pre-existing tanka. Once they place their tanka in its new prose context, meaning is altered and sometimes radically. The presence of tanka, of course, conditions the prose also, but few commentators, in my experience, have paid attention to that circumstance.

Before asking one final question, Jeffrey, I'd like to take this opportunity to thank you for your time and patience in granting me this interview.

That's very gracious of you, Claire, but the pleasure has been mine. Your question?

I have been struck by the diversity of subject matter in my reading of tanka prose, from poignant personal accounts of family life from writers such as Bob Lucky, to the lyrical pieces favoured by Michael McClintock, through to the travelogues composed by writers such as Jane Reichhold and Miriam Sagan, or dramatic, historical accounts such as your own chilling "The Trial of Dorothy Talbye, 1638." There is clearly much scope within this versatile genre. Do you envisage any limits to the possible routes it might take?

I share your assessment of tanka prose, Claire, as wide-ranging. Its boundaries, if circumscribed at all, may coincide largely with the breadth, or lack thereof, of the poetic imagination and skill of the form's practitioners. The norm in contemporary practice, to date, has been a composition of modest length that may be most easily characterized as an abbreviated memoir or confessional anecdote, the crystallization of one significant event or experience in the author's life. Departures from that model do not often involve expansion or greater length but, instead, represent a shift away from a focus on the writer's person in favor of a text that is engaged in literary allusion, in ekphrasis or in what, for lack of a precise term, I might call prose poetry.

One noteworthy exception to this observation can be found in the rapid development, in 2008 and 2009, of an English equivalent of the Japanese poem tale—fictions that lie close, in origin, to folklore and children's stories. An inspiration and model for these attempts can be found in the fairytale-like qualities of the ninth century "Tale of the Bamboo Cutter" (*Taketori monogatari*); they also bear traces of the Brothers Grimm and of the French tales of Charles Perrault and Madame d'Aulnoy. Ingrid Kunschke, in "Thistledown," personifies the wind and, in her brisk opening, establishes a gentle, wistful tone that typifies her contribution to this recent turn in tanka prose:

> That night the wind died down.
>
> I've had enough, he said to himself. Who cares anyway? No one does. Not for me, that is. And he lay down to sleep among the thistles at the far end of the meadow. [21]

Giselle Maya, in "Wild Boars Enchanted," situates the mysterious in the commonplace activities of our daily existence:

> As I was painting ochre pigment onto the walls of my little stone cabanon at dusk, I heard some crackling of branches, as though someone were coming to visit. Sometimes Madame Bosio brings me iris roots or comes with her dog to chat a while . . . .[22]

This touching, personal revelation of the poet in her garden functions as a prelude to her discovery of a family of wild boars who, magically possessed of the power of speech, plead for refuge. A local hunter later catches sight of the matriarch of this boar clan, is transformed into a boar and pleads with the poet for a kiss to reverse the charm. Such is the world of the poem tale in tanka prose!

To look ahead, however, is often to look behind and, in speculating about new avenues for tanka prose tomorrow, to revisit yesterday. In Japan, there are extended histories and biographies, military chronicles and diaries, travelogues and tales. I see no fixed barrier to the ambition of tanka prose in English, no reason why it cannot parallel or rival its classical ancestor in variety and in scale.

Notes

1. Jeffrey Woodward, "A Record of Semimaru," *Modern English Tanka* V2, N2, Winter 2007, p. 174.

2. Jeffrey Woodward, Ed., *The Tanka Prose Anthology*, Modern English Tanka Press, 2008, p. 10.

3. Laurel Rasplica Rodd, *Kokinshū: A Collection of Poems Ancient and Modern*, Cheng & Tsui, 1996, pp. 121-143.

4. *Ibid.*, p. 218.

5. Shiki Masaoka, *Songs from a Bamboo Village,* translated by Sanford Goldstein and Seishi Shinoda. Charles E. Tuttle Co., 1998, p. 247.

6. *Ibid.,* p. 251.

7. Richard Bowring, *Murasaki Shikibu, Her Diary and Poetic Memoirs,* Princeton University Press, 1985, p. 231.

8. Dru Philippou, "Sloughing Off," *Haibun Today* V5, N1, March 2011.

9. Jeffrey Woodward, "Prose and Verse in Tandem: Haibun and Tanka Prose," *Modern Haibun & Tanka Prose 2,* Winter 2009, p. 158, and n. 13, pp. 162-163.

10. Helen Craig McCullough, *Classical Japanese Prose: An Anthology,* Stanford University Press, 1990, pp. 111-112.

11. Edwin A. Cranston, *A Waka Anthology: Volume One The Gem-Glistening Cup,* Stanford Univeristy Press, 1993, p. 309.

12. Michael McClintock, "Before Croissants and Coffee," *Modern Haibun & Tanka Prose 1,* Summer 2009, p. 129.

13. Jeffrey Woodward, "The Elements of Tanka Prose," *Modern English Tanka* V2, N4, Summer 2008, p. 194.

14. Sanford Goldstein, "Not Again! Tanka Strings and Sequences," *Atlas Poetica 5,* Spring 2010, p. 65.

15. Cranston, *op. cit.,* pp. 552-554; Ian Hideo Levy, *The Ten Thousand Leaves: A Translation of the Manyōshū, Volume One,* Princeton University Press, 1981, pp. 371-375; and *1000 Poems from the Manyōshū: The Complete Nippon Gakujutsu Shinkokai Translation,* Dover Publications, 2005, pp. 258-259.

16. Ray Rasmussen, "Terra Incognita: The World of Haibun and Tanka Prose," *Contemporary Haibun Online* V5, N4, December 2009.

17. Meredith McKinney, *The Tale of Saigyō*, Michigan Papers in Japanese Studies, No. 25, Center for Japanese Studies, University of Michigan Press, 1998, p. 35.

18. Bob Lucky, "Three," in *The Tanka Prose Anthology, op. cit.*, p. 76.

19. Jeffrey Woodward, "The Road Ahead for Tanka in English," *Modern English Tanka* V2, N2, Winter 2007, p. 181.

20. Denis M. Garrison, "Dreaming Room," *Modern English Tanka* V1, N3, Spring 2007, p. 4.

21. Ingrid Kunschke, "Thistledown," *Modern Haibun & Tanka Prose 1*, Summer 2009, p. 71.

22. Giselle Maya, "Wild Boars Enchanted," *Haibun Today* (Nov. 26, 2008).

Acknowledgments

The author wishes to acknowledge the following periodicals for first publishing, often in earlier versions, those tanka and tanka prose works reprinted herein: *Atlas Poetica*, *Eucalypt* (Australia), *Haibun Today*, *Lynx*, *Modern English Tanka*, *Modern Haibun & Tanka Prose*, *Moonset*, *Notes from the Gean* (U.K.), *Red Lights*, *Ribbons*, *Santa Fe Poetry Broadside*, *Simply Haiku* and *Skylark* (U.K.).

I am greatly indebted to Denis M. Garrison, of Modern English Tanka Press, for his vital encouragement and support during various projects. My essays, "The Road Ahead for Tanka in English" and "The Elements of Tanka Prose," were first published by him respectively in *Modern English Tanka V2, N2* (Winter 2007) and in *V2, N4* (Summer 2008) while I edited, with his blessing and guidance as my publisher, *The Tanka Prose Anthology* (2008) and *Modern Haibun & Tanka Prose 1-2* (2009).

My thanks are due to M. Kei and his associate editors for regularly selecting my work for the annual series *Take Five: Best Contemporary Tanka*. One tanka, "the road to you," and one tanka prose work, "The Girl from Shanghai," were reprinted in *Volume 1* (2008); two tanka, "the back of the biwa" and "on the river road," in *Volume 3* (2010); and one tanka, "I did not flinch but," in *Volume 4* (2011). I salute M. Kei, also, for soliciting my interview, "Tanka Prose, Tanka Tradition," so ably conducted by Claire Everett and published by Kei in *Atlas Poetica 9* (Summer 2011).

"Glass Lake" and "A Record of Semimaru," two tanka prose compositions previously published elsewhere, were kindly selected by Giselle Maya for her anthology, *Poem Tales* (Saint Martin de Castillon, France: Koyama Press, 2010).

Finally, I want to express my gratitude to Dave Bacharach and Kirsty Karkow, editors of *The Pebbled Shore: The Tanka Society of America's 2009 Anthology*, for publishing my tanka, "I let it go."

About the Author

Jeffrey Woodward, with the exception of abbreviated stints in West Virginia, New Mexico and California, has worked and lived in the Great Lakes Region for much of his life. He graduated with honors from Eastern Michigan University with majors in language arts (linguistics) and political science. His poems and articles appear frequently in periodicals and anthologies throughout North America, Europe and Asia.

Woodward currently acts as general editor of *Haibun Today*, a journal that he founded in 2007. He formerly edited *Modern Haibun & Tanka Prose* and served, in 2010 and again in 2011, as adjudicator for the British Haiku Society's Haiku Awards. His selected poems, under the title *In Passing*, were published in 2007 and he edited *The Tanka Prose Anthology* in 2008.

Colophon

The word *tournesol* is derived from the Italian *girasole*—meaning, "to turn with the sun"—and serves as the common French name for *Helianthus annuus*, Van Gogh's beloved sunflower. The uniform alignment of sunflowers in a field, which supports the false impression that they track the sun, results from heliotropism when the young plants are in bud. Buds maintain this heliotropic motion—a circadian rhythm that is synchronized by the sun, even when obscured on cloudy days—until, with the appearance of mature flower heads, the flowers steadfastly face East.

Tournesol
Detroit • 2013